MINDFUL RELATIONSHIP

HABIT

By: Peter J. Williams

ABOUT THE BOOK

Mindfulness is consists of paying attention to an experience from moment to moment. It is a calm awareness of your consciousness, in the present, without drifting into thoughts of the past or concerns about the future or into opinions about what is going on.

Dr. Dan Siegel believes it results from your reflections on the events of your life and the meaning behind them. The more you make sense of your life, the more you can choose to be free from the nonproductive patterns of the past. More and more evidence is showing that mindfulness can increase your enjoyment of life, your relationships, and your emotional health.

Dan Siegel, a researcher in the neurobiology of relationships, says that taking time to understand ourselves develops a capacity for "Mindsight." - that is, an ability to observe and be aware of the mind itself. Mindsight, the capacity for insight and empathy, can be developed throughout life within our relationships with others and internal reflections about our self.

Being mindful is at the heart of nurturing relationships. When we are mindful, we are aware of our own thoughts and feelings and are also open to those of others. If we have clarity within ourselves, we are more able to fully appreciate the uniqueness of others. Being mindful also helps us to purposefully choose a behavior with the other person's well-being in mind. Others notice our thoughtfulness and feel safe and nurtured around us. Mindfulness thus enhances all of our relationships.

Contrary to what many believe, early experiences do not have to determine your fate. When you are able to make sense of your early experiences, you are more likely to be able forgive yourself and others and are less likely to recreate old patterns. Without self-understanding, science has shown that "history will repeat itself."

Siegel's research in neuroscience suggests that the brain continues to develop both new connections and perhaps new neurons throughout a persons life. The connections among neurons determine how mental processes are created. Experience shapes neural connections in the brain. Therefore, experience shapes the mind. Interpersonal relationships and self-reflection foster the ongoing growth of the mind.

Being mindful helps us to focus on more than just the surface of our experience. We can intentionally

choose to grow; intentionally choose to appreciate others, and therefore intentionally allow new neural networks to develop in the brain. When we do so our living becomes more joyful.

Table of Contents

INTRODUCTION

"If your relationship to the present moment is not right - nothing can ever be right in the future - because when the future comes - it's the present moment." That is a quotation from Eckhart Tolle who was labelled as the most popular spiritual author in the US according to New York Times and an author who was able to sell millions of copies of his books in North America. What the quotation Tolle said is directly related to being mindful. It can be same as saying that if you are not mindful of what is happening now, you would never be ready for what your future has to offer you because eventually, the thing you are labelling as the "future" today would sooner be labelled as your "present". Being mindful is really important in many aspects of your life but before that, we must define what mindfulness is first.

If you are in a classroom filled with people with your professor talking in front about French Revolution while you are playing a game on your cellular phone, you are not mindful of what is happening around the classroom. You are just aware that your professor is discussing something in front and that you are in a classroom but you do not know what is actually going on. Mindfulness is when you know you are there and you exert effort in paying attention to your professor and to what he is saying. If you are mindful, you would be able to answer questions that he might ask you or you would be able to ask questions about the discussion because your interest is there and you have this sense of responsiveness to the situation.

Another example would be having a talk with your best friend. Your best friend asked you to meet her at the nearest coffee shop because she has a problem. When you arrived at the coffee shop, she started crying and she started ranting about her problem. Then, your cell phone beeped signalling that you have a text message from another person. Still, your best friend continues crying and talking but your attention is not drawn into her anymore. You are no longer mindful of all the stuff that she is saying. All you know is that you are responding to a text message and that you have a friend with you who has problems but you do not know what she has been saying since your phone beeped. You may be mindful of what the text message has said but not of the concerns of your best friend. Mindfulness is when you are able to attend to your best friend's problems and if you are able to recognize her feelings during that very moment. By being mindful during that moment, you would be able to give her the advices which are appropriate to her situation.

Last example would be an instance where you see that your mom and dad are fighting but you can hardly hear and understand what they are arguing about. You see them fighting but you do not know what exactly happen. If you are not mindful, you would just immediately think that it is the fault of either your mom or your dad. You would jump into conclusions and you would judge either one of them. Mindfulness is when you are aware that your mom and dad are fighting and you take time to understand why they are arguing. You would not generalize based on your past experiences from them. Instead, you would analyse what is happening and you would not just judge.

Being mindful is putting your attention and care to a certain situation on that same moment during the occurrence of that event and being very critical about all sides of that situation. It is being to recognize the emotions and the deepest corners of that event. It is being able to evaluate and analyse that situation with utmost care and open-mindedness that you have acquired from being mindful during that same circumstance. Being mindful is a cycle. You become mindful about a situation, then, you become educated from it which makes your mind more open and more mindful the next time you get into other situations which require mindfulness.

CHAPTER 1

THE MIND

The human mind has been a subject of interest to many people all over the world since ages. Many of the scientists and doctors have been studying this subject called mind from hundreds of years. But still there is a lot of mystery to be unfolded. But man has realized that the ultimate power of this universe lies in the human mind. We all know the fact that the technology and scientific development that we see today is a result of the powerful human mind. The human mind has changed everything in this universe.

Now, if we go deep inside the mind there is a lot to be still unfolded. The complete power of the human mind has not been exploited till date. Many of the psychotherapists say that the actual potential of a human being lies in the subconscious mind. This subconscious mind is the ultimate powerhouse of the human being. It records each and everything of your life and dictates habitual patterns. This is the reason why man has to be completely aware of the content of his subconscious mind. If the subconscious mind is filled with positive things, the human being attracts all the positive situations in his life. But if the subconscious mind is negative then there are chances that the human being ends up in negativity.

This way, the mind plays a fairly vital role in shaping a person's life. Waking up to the full potential of this mind will definitely change the person's life in leaps and bounds. The mind can be used as a weapon to attain progress and to live a life which is always happy. For that you need to first of all understand the structure of the mind and then go into the nature of working of the human mind. Your mind has the capacity of attracting what it wants. This is the reason why it can be said that the situations that you are experiencing right now in your life have been attracted to you. You need to be very careful when you are conditioning your subconscious mind. If you're conditioning it in a positive affirmative way your life will be filled with all positive situations.

So start sowing seeds of positivity in your subconscious mind and change your life. You mind gets what you want. All thoughts that have gone into your subconscious mind come out as your conscious action. If you set goals, your subconscious mind will make them accomplished. So all you need to do is ask your subconscious mind and get them done.

This is the reason why mind is considered as the most powerful weapon in this whole universe. Use your mind in the right way and you'll get the right results. Control your thoughts and give positive suggestions to your subconscious mind and fill your life with positive situations. The mind has unlimited power when it comes to making things happen. Whenever you find some time, use it to completely relax your mind. Never fill your mind with negativity, jealousy, hatred, violence and so on. This will go a long way when it comes to controlling your thoughts and filling your life it complete positivity. With a calm mind you can achieve anything- may it be a goal or ultimate salvation.

What is Mindfulness?

Mindfulness means paying attention in a particular way, on purpose, in the present moment, non-judgmentally.

Mindfulness, a state of alertness in which the mind does not get caught up in thoughts, emotions, desires or sensations, but lets them come and go, much like watching a river flow by.

Mindfulness is nonjudgmental observation: It is that ability of the mind to observe without criticism. When mindful, one sees things without condemnation or judgment. One does not decide and does not judge. One just observes.

Mindfulness is non-egotistic alertness. It takes place without reference to self. With mindfulness one sees all phenomena without references to concepts like "me," "my," or "mine." decide and does not judge. One just observes.

Mindfulness is cultivated through meditation. It is a practice.

Benefits of Mindfulness

Mindfulness meditation practice can be transformative. It has been shown scientifically to have diverse and far-reaching impacts, and has the potential to transform the way we respond to life events.

• It reduces stress and negative emotional reactivity.

• It reduces psychopathology.

• It heightens attention and awareness.

• It promotes self-actualization.

• It enables seeing opportunities for open, spontaneous action in the world, free from egoism

Mindfulness in Society

Mindfulness meditation is becoming widely recognized as an effective tool for mental and physical health. For example in the States, the National Institutes of Health (NIH) is financing more than 50 studies testing mindfulness techniques - up from 3 in the year 2000 - to help relieve stress, soothe addictive cravings, improve attention, lift despair.

Mindfulness and the military: Coping with stress

In one study just published in the journal Emotion by Amishi Jha and her colleagues persuaded 48 Marines who were headed to Iraq to participate in their scientific study.

During a full eight weeks before deployment, one group of 31 Marines spent two practiced regular mindfulness meditation while another group of 17 men had no mindfulness training.

Jha wanted to know if mindfulness would improve soldiers' ability to control emotion by improving working memory capacity. The reasoning behind this was the idea that working memory capacity may not just helps manage information in reasoning and problem solving - but it might also help manage emotion and keep the brain functioning well under stress. This is a type of emotional intelligence.

The stress of deployment did - as expected - decrease the Marines' working memory capacity. But those who practiced mindfulness for longer periods actually saw a slight increase in working memory capacity.

Compared with soldiers who didn't have the training, the 'mindful' Marines also experienced more positive moods and fewer negative moods.

Take home: Build fluid intelligence and shield it from stress with mindfulness meditation and working memory training.

Mindfulness could benefit people who are in similar situations to the military - those who require periods of intensive physical, mental and emotional demands on the job, such as firefighters, police officers, other first responders and crisis workers, the researchers say.

But more generally, mindfulness meditation can help shield cognitive functioning and the exercise of our fluid intelligence under conditions of stress. Let's face it: life is stressful - whether taking exams, or dealing with cognitive pressures at work! If the meditation is combined with brain training that our company supplies, we have a powerful training combination.

I personally have for a long time combined working memory training with mindfulness meditation. These results come as a nice vindication of something I've experienced to be highly valuable for more than a year now. I've understand for a long time that our intelligence is not just about information processing - it is also about smart with our emotions.

CHAPTER 2

<u>MINDFULNESS IN RELATIONSHIPS</u>

Practice mindfulness in your relationships and all your virtuous qualities will blossom. Mindfulness, derived from Buddhist tradition, involves focused attention on, and awareness of, your bodily sensations, reactions to internal and external stimuli, and the fluctuating thoughts that pass through your mind. If you practice mindfulness consistently, your mind/body system cannot help but live virtuously. That is, you will naturally develop and live with virtuous qualities such as patience, kindness, humility, integrity, charity, pure thinking and a balanced and even tempered disposition.

Mindfulness is often practiced as a meditation. You create a comfortable, distraction-free environment. You sit or stand, remain still or walk, in an upright, strong and relaxed posture. You gaze downward focusing a couple of inches in front of you nose. Your eyes are open and soft. You notice your breathing, observe it and allow its movement in and out, and you watch yourself become increasingly relaxed. You notice your thoughts and decide not to pay attention to them right now, maybe later, and you bring your awareness and focus back into yourself.

Even among people who practice mindfulness alone, once they are joined with a partner or in a business, friendship, family or intimate relationship, they may revert back to habitual habit patterns. All those virtues can disappear if we discontinue the mindful practice in relationship with others. We may become impatient, we may lose our temper, we may forget to be kind or generous, or start thinking negative or judgemental thoughts.

Mindfulness practice must become a way of living, an every day, moment to moment experience. Being mindful in your everyday interactions with an intimate partner can be an enlightening, freeing and totally loving experience. When we are mindful, nobody is required to change anything. We just observe, allow, and appreciate the reality of what appears to exist right now.

Here are some steps to help you practice mindfulness in your relationships.

1. Observation: Observe your self, your partner and others, moment to moment.

2. Awareness: Become aware of your internal and external environment. Notice your own sensations, thoughts, beliefs, attitudes, and

responses to others. Notice the attitudes, words and actions of others.

3. Description: Describe the details that you are observing and continue to describe the details of what you are becoming increasingly aware of.

4. Nonjudgemental: Notice your judgements, your criticisms, your critiques of yourself and others. Continue to release and let go of any judgements that you notice. Let your thoughts be pure.

5. Nonreaction: Accept, allow, strive to understand, forgive human frailties in yourself and others. Develop a broader, more inclusive and higher perspective

Take an inventory now of your own thoughts, beliefs, attitudes and responses to others. Do you often take the time to step back and just observe? Are you consciously aware of internal and external stimuli and your own automatic responses? Do you consciously describe what you are observing and feeling without judgment or reaction?

Imagine being mindful, moment to moment, in your most significant relationships. Imagine being mindful in your everyday encounters with other people. Imagine how you might feel, moment to moment, living in a continuous state of mindfulness.

CHAPTER **3**

INFORMAL AND FORMAL MINDFULNESS TRAINING

Mindfulness is best described as moment-by-moment awareness. There are four dimensions of mindful moments. They are

(1) present centered, (2) non-judgmental, (3) non-verbal, and (4) non-conceptual.

Mindful moments always focus on the present, never the past or the future. Most thoughts are one step removed from the present moment because they focus on the past or future. Mindful moments always exist in the present space and time, a context often referred to as the "here and now." Mindfulness revolves around being fully involved in the here and now. Mindful moments are not thinking moments where you try to figure something out or judge it. Mindful moments are non-conceptual because during them you merely note the occurrence of something and accept it for what it is. You do not judge what you are experiencing, you accept it. The talking that goes on during mindful moments is self-talk. It is non-verbal and also known as sub-vocal speech. Essentially self-talk is what you say to yourself when thinking or feeling something. When people describe or write down self-talk messages it adds an additional layer of interpretation and distance from them. Mindfulness is developed through informal and formal training activities.

Informal mindfulness training revolves around the application of mindful behavior into daily experience. Informal mindfulness training involves learning how to devote your full attention to every activity you are engaged in. There are two dimensions of informal mindfulness training; (1) becoming more mindful of your internal environment (thoughts, feelings, mental images), and (2) becoming more aware of your external environment (behavior and immediate physical surroundings).

Becoming more aware of your internal environment is the first step in accepting it and co-existing with it as you work towards accomplishing tasks and meeting your goals. Being more mindful of the things going on in your internal environment is different from judging or evaluating them. When you are truly mindful of your thoughts you notice them without judgment. It is as if you have stepped outside of your own mind and are looking at your thoughts as an outside observer of them. When you do this you'll probably notice that a lot of your thoughts and feelings are not very helpful in meeting your goals and living a life based on your values. One of the keys to stress management is living our lives according to our values and standards and the goals we set based on these things. A key to doing this is understanding when our thoughts are not helpful because they are really judgments and evaluations instead of observations about the present moment.

Becoming more aware of your external environment revolves around increasing your awareness of your behavior and what's going on in your immediate physical surroundings as you engage in this behavior.

Mindful eating is often used as a form of external mindfulness training. It focuses on your eating behavior and the context in which it occurs, your immediate physical environment. Mindful eating is often taught to people with eating disorders to help them become more mindful of their eating behavior. When you practice mindful eating you sit quietly at a table slowly pick up small pieces of food with your utensils, gradually lift the food off your plate and bring it to your mouth, and take slow bites chewing thoroughly. For those engaged in the practice, they experience eating like never before. They are taught to pay attention to the presentation of the food before eating it- the color, shape, placement, aromas, etc. They begin to marvel at things like how the fingers, hands, and arms work in consort with their brain to pick the food up and bring it into the mouth, the process of chewing, the experience of tasting something anew.

Formal mindfulness training is a structured program of daily practice of mindfulness meditation sessions. These sessions are in addition to continuing informal mindfulness training through mindful eating, walking etc. Generally you would begin by meditating for a few minutes three to four times a week. After a couple of weeks of this you would increase the duration of your sessions by five minutes and repeat this until you could meditate for 20-30 minutes at a time.

CHAPTER 4

<u>MINDFULNESS MEDITATION- HEALTH CARE FOR YOU</u>

Mindfulness meditation is free. There are no health insurance premiums, drug costs, or expensive therapies. And it works! But first you have to understand the authentic instructions, and secondly you must practice diligently. If you do this, mental and physical problems will melt away. Try it! How can you lose?

To begin with, each of the 8 steps below may take a day, a week, a month, even a year before you are confident in your grasp of that particular step. But before you become impatient, remember that building a good foundation by not rushing from step to step will pay off big time later. If you practice only step one, fully, with confidence and awareness, it will lead to total liberation from stress, and eventual "enlightenment."

But rushing from step to step, trying to hurry the process and get somewhere quickly, results in nothing but restlessness and boredom. There will be no internal shifts, no AHA! moments, which are those experiences that can occur in any of the steps if the step is practiced deeply enough. It's these moments of split second insight, these experiences of 'other worldliness' that are so important for unshakable faith to develop the

39

practice. Remember; this is not a belief system, this is unquestionable personal experience.

Whatever you do, please don't make meditation a stressful exercise. Relax in all aspects of it. If you are too tight, if you concentrate too hard trying to attain this or that, stress will develop instead of calm. Let go, let go, let go.

Conversely, if you are too lax and simply drift through your practice haphazardly and casually with only feeble attempts to concentrate and calm the mind, no penetrating wisdom will result. The depth of your mind's concentration, sharpness, calmness and a knack for randomly seeing "what is' in each moment, are what determine the resulting quality of the mind's insight and wisdom, which then leads directly to a stress-free life.

In other words, there will be no abandonment, no disinterest, no dispassion or understanding about the things, circumstances and people that are currently the objects of your stress. Without this disenchantment and relinquishment, deeper states of meditation are not possible.

There will be no transition from the world dominated mind to the free, spiritual being because the mind is simply too entangled in the wrong ways with worldly concerns. There may be perceived spiritual progress, but only the spiritual progress that you imagine. What you do and think about constantly all day and night are the real indicators of where you are and where you are headed.

So, how do we put this all together in a practice that leads to a new understanding of life and a reduction of stress?

There are two basic meditation techniques presently practiced by most meditators. One is called concentration meditation, (jhana), and the other is called wisdom or insight meditation (vipassana), which is nowadays called 'mindfulness meditation.'

The method described here combines both, and is based on the actual suttas of the Buddha, not the commentaries or ideas of those that followed the Buddha. It therefore combines concentration and wisdom as the Buddha laid out 2550 years ago in his Anapanasati Sutta, indicating that concentration and insight are inseparable.

This method however does not advocate practicing the methods separately - practicing one method (concentration) for awhile, and then practicing the other (insight or mindfulness meditation) for awhile, as is presently practiced by many Buddhists. The method described below practices both concentration and insight at the same time.

Therefore, your practice is balanced at all times. This not only makes the practice tranquil and non-stressful, but naturally results in eventual deep insights into the mind and body that can occur rather quickly, providing that the correct kind of effort and time is devoted to the practice.

STEP 1. Thought Awareness

In order to establish a firm foundation in your meditation, begin by practicing simple "thought awareness."

Thoughts about what you did yesterday, what you will do tomorrow or next year, how much longer the meditation session will last! What you will do after meditation, or about that itch, or having to swallow all the time. All these thoughts can ambush you.

When thoughts do steal your attention, where you become involved in them rather than being mindful that you are thinking, you lose your awareness. When this happens, be kind to the thought that stole your attention - but not too kind.

Allow each thought to have its space without angrily pushing it away, but at the same time, shift your focus from the content of thought, or what you were thinking about, to the feeling of the thought. You will feel a tension in the brain when you are thinking, even thinking so called happy thoughts. It's subtle, but the tension can be discovered with some practice.

Thought is a conflict solver. So, when you are thinking you are naturally in conflict. Thinking how to balance your checkbook, or what you have to do tomorrow, or even thinking about how you can get people to like or respect you - this is all conflict. Fear of running out of money, becoming unpopular or disrespected, getting something you crave but can't have, or putting up with something you dislike and can't get rid of - these are objects of thought where thinking tries to resolve the situation by figuring it all out.

So while we are practicing, we no longer participate any further in a thought once we realize that we are thinking. We stop trying to figure things out, or indulging in the content of our thoughts, regardless of how important it is that you solve whatever conflict the thought is trying to resolve, or the plans it is trying to complete.

When you continue to think, after you are mindful that you should be meditating - that is not good meditation. On the other hand, noticing thoughts, gently letting them be and returning to your mindfulness of thought awareness - this is good meditation, even if you have to do it a million times.

Noticing how mind works

When you find yourself caught up in a thought and then successfully let go of the contents of the thought, take one more step: Take a moment to realize the attachment you have for this particular thought (it seems very real and important to you).

Then notice how that attachment causes stress, and how the more important a thought seems, the more stress it causes.

This noticing and realization does not come about by thinking some more about the thought and our attachment to it, but by merely experiencing the feeling of stress or tension that the thought causes in our brain. Then, we experience how that tension releases when we let go of the tight grasp the mind has on that thought.

This is how you will begin to acquire wisdom about how the mind works. You will also discover what your attachments and aversions are. In addition, you may discover how a "self" is fabricated from thought, and therefore our 'self' is nothing more than a mirage. Eventually, after practicing this way for some time, we can let go of our assumed self importance, which is the cause of most of our stress.

This is how vipassana (insight) is developed within the tranquil jhana (concentration) practice, and how mindfulness meditation develops.

So to recap: When your mindfulness remembers that you are thinking about something instead of simply being aware of the thinking mind, there is a tendency to quickly push the thought away, hating it, considering it to be a hindrance to your meditation, and then quickly jumping back to your object of meditation, which is simple thought awareness.

Instead of quickly pushing the thought away, however, take a moment and apply your mindfulness to the grasping, the feeling of tightness that the thought has caused the mind. Don't think about the content of the thought itself, just notice the feeling in the mind that it has caused. The thought seems very important to the mind because something either has to be resolved, or we are trying to think how to position ourselves so that we are more liked, admired, respected, secure, happy, etc.

So, the mind is either trying to solve a conflict, or trying to build the idea of "me " and "mine" - reinforcing the "I" thought. But you don't have to think about all of this or try to figure it out. Simply notice the tension that thought creates.

Then release that tension. Release the grasp that the mind has on that particular thought. You will feel your temples and eye muscles physically relax when you do this.

Then allow the mind to expand, releasing itself from the confines of the brain. Let it expand as far as it likes, out toward unlimited space.

Now take a deep breath, and as you exhale, relax the body, let the arms fall from the shoulders, relax the face and abdomen.

Now happily notice your uninterrupted awareness of the mind without thoughts, as long as you can.

Again, here's what you do when you find the mind is distracted in thought:

A. Apply your mindfulness to the grasping, the feeling of tightness

B. Then release that tension.

C. Then allow the mind to expand

D. Now take a deep breath, and as you exhale, relax the body

Insight into how the mind works is not a result of the brain trying to figure all of this out. Insight comes as a flash, after which perfect understanding prevails. No need to keep reading more books or practicing anything other than keeping your mindfulness and awareness as an anchor, watching thoughts come and go. You are now an observer, not a doer. Eventually, if one wants to go deep into jhana and vipassana practice, the controller, the doer, must go.

All the wisdom of the universes and beyond is inside the mind. All you have to do is calm the mind, then direct it toward avenues other than those which you have been traveling all your life until that innate wisdom has a chance to surface.

Practice this Step 1 until your thoughts slow down to the extent that you can catch each and every one and apply 'A' through 'D' below:

A. Apply your mindfulness to the grasping, the feeling of tightness

B. Then release that tension.

C. Then allow the mind to expand

D. Now take a deep breath, and as you exhale, relax the body, and go back to standing on the beach.

Then go on to step 2, but don't hurry step 1!

STEP 2. Gaps between thoughts

As you practice, thoughts settle down becoming less frequent. You will then notice gaps between your thoughts. These are brief moments where there is an anticipation of what comes next, as if the mind suddenly has become empty of thoughts and you find yourself ready to ambush the next thought that comes your way.

Keep practicing this way until the periods between thoughts lengthen. Don't go to STEP 3 until just the image of the empty mind, without thoughts, can be maintained for about five minutes.

STEP 3. Noticing the body breathing in the silent gaps between thoughts.

At some point within these gaps between thoughts, and simply because nothing else is going on, the mind will begin noticing that the body is breathing, It will notice the in breaths and the out breaths. It doesn't matter where you notice this breathing, you just notice it. You just know that the body is breathing.

Stay with this awareness of breathing in and breathing out Stay with this noticing as long as you can before you find yourself caught in a thought. Keep doing this breath awareness until the mind can remain mindful of the breath for about 20 uninterrupted minutes with no or few thoughts, before moving to STEP 4.

STEP 4. Now we will begin following the Buddha's actual instructions on mindfulness of breathing, or the Anapanassati Sutta.

"There is the case where a monk having gone to the wilderness to the shade of a tree or to or an empty building sits down folding his legs crosswise holding his body erect and setting mindfulness before everything."

Get into the best posture you can, one that you will be able to maintain for the entire length of your meditation period without moving. The best position is the full lotus posture where you place your right foot on top of your left thigh, and your left foot on top of your right thigh. This is only for very flexible people! Keep in mind that all meditation positions have to be worked at for some time to become comfortable, and in the meantime there will be some pain.

Another good position is the half lotus, where the right foot is placed on the left thigh. Most statues and pictures of the Buddha depict this position.

Burmese style is also very good where the feet are not placed on top of the thighs but laid out in front of them. There are pictures of these sitting positions under the "Fundamentals of Buddhism" tab.

Sitting on a chair is okay as well, just sit with your back straight but relaxed, and don't lean back.

The important thing with all of these postures is to eventually put mindfulness of breathing before everything else. This means being able to sit comfortably, upright, and stable for long periods of time where you are involved only in your breathing rather than getting caught up in moving the body around and fidgeting.

Now, put your mindfulness completely on the breath and go to STEP 5.

STEP 5. Detailed breath awareness

" Breathing in long, he discerns, 'I am breathing in long'; or breathing out long, he discerns, 'I am breathing out long.' Or breathing in short, he discerns, 'I am breathing in short'; or breathing out short, he discerns, 'I am breathing out short."

Simply know detailed aspects of each in breath and out breath as you are breathing - whether it is long or short, shallow or deep, fast or slow, or calm or stressful. You can become aware of the length of the breath by how long it takes to inhale and exhale. One way is to see if the inhales and exhales are equal, or whether one is longer than the other. Another way is to see how calm and relaxed the breath can become. If you notice your breathing is tight and constricted, try to loosen or relax it. Play with the breath and see how many subtleties you can detect.

Do this until you can notice the beginning, middle and end of each in breath, and the beginning, middle and end of each out breath for about 20 minutes without intervening thoughts.

STEP 6. Body awareness

"He trains himself, 'I will breathe in sensitive to the entire body'". He trains himself, 'I will breathe out sensitive to the entire body.'"

Here we will begin two exercises which will open and familiarize us with the energy centers of the body (and all the while remembering to keep all the in breaths and out breaths in mind in the background). The in breaths and out breaths become our anchor, our "go to" guy when we find ourselves losing our awareness of that mindfulness that the Buddha said is to take priority over everything else.

The first exercise harmonizes the body and can protect it from illness. The second harmonizes both body and mind and keeps the meditation practice stable and balanced.

Begin with a deep inhalation at your tailbone and visualize it moving up your spine to the top of your head (in a seemingly counter intuitive fashion). Then let the exhale fall over your chest like a waterfall and around the pelvic area before you begin another circling inhalation at your tailbone. Do this three times. Be sure to relax your body fully on the out breath - allow you arms and face to fall. Relax the belly, let it hang out! This is the first exercise, which takes about 30 seconds.

After your three circling breaths, the second exercise involves putting your attention on the energy centers of the body, or the 'chakras:' This one takes about a minute:

Calmly breathe in and out two times from the forehead area just between and above the eyebrows. Imagine this forehead area, as well as all the organs in this area, opening and expanding.

Now do the same at the throat - the hollow area below your Adam's Apple - breathe in and out two times and imagine this area and all the organs in this area opening and expanding.

Now do the same at the heart - the center of the chest.

Next the solar plexus, or an area 2" above your belly button.

Next the pubic area.

Then the tailbone area.

And finally bring the breath around the back to about 2" above the top of the head.

1. Forehead

2. Throat

3. Heart

4. Solar plexus

5. Pubic area

6. Tailbone

7. Top of head

It is recommended that these two short excises be practiced before each meditation session.

STEP 7. Tranquilizing the body

"He trains himself, 'I will breathe in calming bodily fabrication (breath).' He trains himself, 'I will breathe out calming bodily fabrication (breath)."

Now simply watch the in breaths and out breaths. Make sure that you know the beginning, middle and end of each in breath, the beginning, middle and end of each out breath. Don't concentrate too hard. Just sit there completely relaxed and calmly know the different parts of each breath. Try not to miss any part or any breath. If you do lose attention, that's okay. Just go back and begin again.

As you are doing this, occasionally think "Easy, calm, relaxed," and your breath will calm all by itself.

If the meditation is done properly with the correct emphasis on 'relaxed, and with consistent effort, the mind will increasingly calm down until the sensation of breathing becomes very refined and almost unnoticeable. Many other things can happen as well, as mind begins to explore amazingly interesting regions it never knew existed.

Do this for as long as you can until the breath either disappears, or a bright light appears right in front of the (closed) eyes. It is good to consult a qualified teacher at this point, as signs and experiences can be misinterpreted.

STEP 8. First jhana

"He trains himself, 'I will breathe in sensitive to rapture.' He trains himself, 'I will breathe out sensitive to rapture.'

Step 8 is really not a step but a result of Steps 1 through 7. Now your mind is catching on to deeper mental states, and it becomes engrossed! This is the beginning of deep shifts in consciousness and understanding. This is the beginning of the jhanas.

There is nothing you can do directly to bring these on. As a matter of fact, trying to bring them on will ruin them because they are very subtle states. The mind alone decides when it is ready for them. All you can do is the above practices wholeheartedly and see what happens, not expecting or anticipating anything. Then, when the mind begins to drop into jhanas, let it drive the car. Just sit back, relax, and enjoy the scenery. The mind itself will find its way through all of the jhanas if you can learn to let it lead without your "self" doing anything.

When the mind is ready to go into these deeper states, it will do so by itself, as was stated. You must let go of all control now. Don't do anything except be mindful and aware. Allow the mind its space to follow its instincts. Trying to do anything except be aware at this level will stop all progress. The thinking, intellectual mind is much too gross to live in the same world as jhanas.

The first indications that the mind is going into beginning jhanic stages are physical feelings of "rapture." Initial feelings of rapture are usually physical, and can include, but not limited to, goose bumps, hair standing on end, extraordinary feelings of freedom or release, and many more.

In the beginning, the problem is that when one is not accustomed to this rapture, there is a tendency to think, "Wow! What was that!" Then of course, that grossness of mind will immediately take the mind out of jhana. Then you will spend the next three months (or years) thinking about the rapture and trying to duplicate the experience instead of letting go and doing the indirect practice that originally brought it on.

So it takes some experience before you can relax into the joy that rapture provides.

Once you can relax into that joy, still always keeping the breath in mind in the background, mind will want to go into deeper stages than merely rapture, which it begins to see as too coarse for the sensitive states that will follow. This is the point where the mind will begin to slide into second jhana.

Here is the stage in your practice where a good teacher with experience in jhanas becomes invaluable, just because it is not easy to know which way to go in practice. There might be a hundred different ways for the mind to go, with only one being the way towards enlightenment. Visions, lights, nimittas, effort, mindfulness, view - all these things and many more need to be explored and understood.

So this is good for now. If you can get this far, enlightenment is not so very far away. It's always up to you.

CHAPTER 5

MINDFULNESS FAMILY - MAKING A RELATIONSHIP WORK

It's said, "A family that prays together stays together." There's probably more truth in that statement than meets the eye. Family cohesiveness needs glue to hold it together. Whether it's prayer or another form of communication, the recipe for a mindfulness relationship resides in taking responsibility.

When two people decide to have a relationship, each person must take 100% responsibility to make the relationship work. When one person slips below taking full responsibility, problems occur. Simply stated, both parties do for their relationship the things they know will enhance the relationship, not harm it.

Whether the relationship is with a friend or a lover, watch what happens when the relationship is working and when it is not. Anything less than taking 100% responsibility for making the relationship work cheats the relationship and throws it off-balance. One person is happy, and the other is not. When both parties take full responsibility, the relationship hums like a fine-tuned motor, and it runs smoothly. In a mindfulness relationship, people communicate a sense of contentment and happiness.

When each person takes 100% responsibility to make a relationship work, it works (period). That does not mean each person takes full responsibility for making the other person happy. Happiness is each person's responsibility, not his/her partner's. How often do you hear a man or woman say, "I did everything I possibly could to make my wife/husband happy, and nothing I did was ever enough!" Happiness comes from within, and it's not something someone can give.

Respect and admiration are things a person can give in a mindfulness relationship. They are ingredients to ensure a feeling of happiness because people enjoy being respected and admired. Interestingly enough, taking full responsibility for communicating respect for a partner is a reflection on how much a person respects their self. A person with little respect for their self can hardly be expected to communicate respect for a partner. So, in a relationship if you find a lack of respect from a partner, it's probably because the partner lacks respect for their self.

The same example can be applied to communicating admiration and taking responsibility for admiring a partner in a relationship. In other words, a person can love, admire and respect another as much as he/she loves, admires and respects their self.

The elusiveness of love is a never-ending chase. It's evident by the divorce statistics in America for marriage. According to DivorceStatistics.org, for first marriages - 45% to 50% of first marriages end in divorce. Second marriages - 60% to 67% of second marriages end in divorce. Third marriages - 70% - 73% of third marriages end in divorce. Couples with children divorce at about a 40% rate vs. couples without children divorce at about a rate of 66%.

People get married and divorced everyday. It's obvious by the divorce rate, and the innovative concept of mindfulness divorce being introduced by cutting-edge lawyers.

Mindfulness divorce is a fairly new concept. According to Thurman Arnold III, and taken from his website, ThurmanArnold.com:

"Mindfulness allows perspective based upon the Truth of our experience, not some trance-talking story about it all. For purposes of divorce, mindfulness begins by recognizing what is mindlessness and the forms of thinking and behavior that mindlessness takes. Mindfulness is being present at any given moment, in a conscious way.... Ultimately it is a practice and a commitment borne of desire, love and patience. "

At the beginning of a new relationship or bringing closure to a mature relationship, stick to the truth because it's the special few who take responsibility and enjoy the pleasure of a mindfulness family experience.

CHAPTER 6

REKINDLE YOUR RELATIONSHIP WITH MINDFULNESS

Too often in a long-term relationship partners stop the very behaviors that connected them with one another and not because they stop loving each other but because they begin to take the other one for granted. Sensual and gratifying behaviors are lost, such as looking deeply into one another's eyes, mouth to mouth kisses, sexual innuendo, offering your partner focused attention, active listening, random compliments, gifts, etc.

What is it that you have stopped doing? What has your partner stopped doing? What behaviors would you like to rekindle in your relationship?

How can Mindfulness help you rekindle your relationship?

Mindfulness is a practice of awareness in the present moment. Dr. John Gottman, relationship expert and researcher, describes successful long-term unions as a "string of pearls" made up of mindful moments of connection and appreciation. The happiest and healthiest couples do not necessarily spend a lot of time in conversation but they have a myriad of ways of mindfully connecting with one another in the present moment.

Walton and Kathryn were a couple who maintained mindful connection for 60 years despite financial hardship, two jobs, and four children. Their laughter was their prosperity during hard times. Their joy and pleasure in one another was the wealth in poverty. Their love was the antidote to sorrow.

Their daughter, Jan, shared that she thought all parents went to sleep laughing and sharing affection at night because her bedroom shared a common wall with her parents'. Joy and laughter are forms of mindful connection to one another in the present moment.

When Walton was dying, he told a group of us who stopped by the story of how he and Kathryn had a hurried wedding so he could go off to the Second World War and that she was still his sweetheart after 60 years. She sat beside him and beamed. Walton and Kathryn are an inspirational couple who maintained a mindful connection over time. We have all seen such couples but what lessons can we apply to our relationships?

In order to have a relationship as successful as theirs, mindful training is a plus. Mindful training includes practice of focusing on the breath to calm down and experience the present moment, and deliberately sending compassion to self and others.

In order to maintain a healthy relationship, partners should make a habit to manifest affection towards one another. Physical affection boosts testosterone in a woman and oxytocin in a man and increases his bonding with her. Just mindfully thinking about your partner with feelings of loving-kindness can boost the pleasure chemical dopamine and lower stress hormones adrenalin and cortisol. You get a kind of pleasurable chemical shower.

One of the most effective acts is mindfully kissing on the mouth. That is because lips are incredibly sensitive. "Of the 12 or 13 cranial nerves that affect cerebral functions, five are at work when we kiss". (Scientific American). In addition, kissing on the mouth allows for exchange of saliva that can help boost the immune system of both partners. Human beings are wired for connection, so practice mindfully bringing yourself into the present moment to enjoy all the sensations generated by an intimate kiss.

In order to maintain a healthy relationship, partners should make a habit to share affection daily. Physical affection boosts testosterone in a woman and oxytocin in a man and increases his bonding with her. Sex therapist, David Schnarch, recommends a type of mindful intimate connection called "eyes open" sex so couples maintain prescient awareness of one another during the sexual experience.

PRACTICES
Physical affection and sex offer a myriad of opportunities to practice mindfulness with your partner.

As you kiss on the lips, notice how your body feels as you attend to the sensations of the present moment.

Remember what behaviors you had when you first fell in love and mindfully repeat those behaviors.

Mindfully look into your partner's eyes with compassion for his/her struggles.

Find ways to connect mindfully with your partner in the present moment through laughter, mutual memories, walks, and shared affection. This becomes a positive bank account of emotions so, when times are hard, you have these connections.

Initiate sexual contact and use all your senses to experience the moment. Look into your partner's eyes, play special music, savor the touch of skin, smell scented candles or massage oil. Always return to the sensations of the present moment.

It is possible to mindfully cultivate a compassionate awareness of your partner by following these steps:

Sit quietly for five minutes at a time and pay attention to your breathing. Since mindfulness is a practice, it is better to do this for longer. However, short segments can also be helpful.

Feel the breath moving into your heart with kindness and care and repeat: "May I be free of suffering. May I be at peace". Allow yourself to be healed. Continue repeating "May I be healed. May I be free of suffering" with each breath.

Imagine loving kindness with each breath. Continue breathing as you focus on your loving kindness and relating to yourself with tenderness while sending well-being into your mind and body. Repeat for a number of breaths: "May I find my greatest joy. May I heal into my true nature".

Now bring your mind to your partner and imagine that you can send them warmth and kindness. With each breath think, "May you be free of suffering. May you be at peace.". Continue the breathing of connection and this wish for their happiness and wholeness, repeating: "May you be free of suffering. May you know your deepest joy, your greatest peace.". Continue and picture your partner's presence with a wish for their healing and deepest joy.

To rekindle your relationship, mindfully pay attention and treat your partner as you treated him/her in the beginning. Don't take him/her for granted and most important: enjoy moments spent together, living it in the present. This is what mindfulness is about!

CHAPTER 7

RELATIONSHIP OF SEX AND STRESS

Have you ever wondered that the role of testosterone in enhancing libido and enhancing erections in men cannot be its only role? There are many other roles and biological effects of testosterone other than its known presence in bodily fluids. It has been blamed for excess hair loss (medical name-Androgenetic alopecia) although the molecular mechanisms of hair loss in men and women are not fully understood.

This hormone testosterone is secreted in the testes of males and the ovaries of females, although men produce more of it. Various kinds of mental behavior are not only subject to influence by environment and genetics but also day-to-day hormonal changes. For example, stress can also inhibit testosterone synthesis and hence lead to decreased levels of it secretion. Levels of sex hormones and the system of stress also affect women in the longer periods such as in menstrual period, pregnancy, and menopause and during the use of oral contraceptives. In depressed women, body levels of estrogen are lower and levels of androgens increased, while the testosterone levels are reduced in depressed men.

Some great findings have recently emerged from scientific studies. Recent studies have shown that to keep stress at bay you should frequently engage in penetrative penal-vaginal sex. Unfortunately many people from all walks of life find that under stress, they do not have the desire to have sex and even creates undesirable side effects such as sexual dysfunction.

A brilliant study (Biological Psychology, volume 71, page 214) showed that sex but more preferably intercourse is much more effective in combating stress then other sexual activity such as masturbation. As intercourse is more linked with less blood pressure and less stress this cause's better psychological and physiological function. Also orgasms for women during penile-vaginal intercourse are better for physiological behavior but not so much for orgasm during other sexual activities. As some of us are nervous about speaking in public or stage fright as it's commonly called, they are being recommended to have sex (not on the stage of course) for the stress calming effect.

It is thought that when a couple makes love the neurotransmitter oxytocin released relaxes the body and decreases blood pressure hence also preventing stress. Oxytocin is secreted by the brain and other organs including the ovaries and testes. It is present in higher levels in women than in men. It is believed that oxytocin is significantly decreased during the stress and infusion of the hormone relieves stress in animal models. This suggests a role in regulating some physiological responses to stress.

In the light of such elegant studies and lack of public stress programmes such as screening by government agencies aimed at improving recognition, treatment, and reducing stress and depression primary; prevention has become necessary. As stress and depression has become a common disorder with serious many unwanted side effects both in men and women, penetrative penal-vaginal sex could be a primary stress prevention strategy.

CHAPTER 8

GETTING PEACE OF MIND IN RELATIONSHIPS

As women, we love relationships! But how often do you find yourself asking "How do I get peace of mind relationships?" I mean, they can cause our greatest joys and our greatest heartbreaks! It can be quite a roller coaster if we're not careful. Today, I'd like to share a simple process for keeping your sanity with the more "difficult to get along with" variety of relationships...

How Do I Get Peace of Mind in Relationships Tip #1:

Accept that your way of looking at things is only one perspective. It's real easy for us to get locked into our belief and refuse to see the world from another vantage point. We make assumptions about why people do things every day that may be totally off base! Just because someone gives you a dirty look, doesn't mean they're mad at you. Perhaps the sun with in his/her eyes. Maybe his/her stomach was hurting!! You just don't KNOW unless you've outright asked.

How Do I Get Peace of Mind in Relationships Tip #2:

Acknowledge the elephant in the room. If you feel a relationship is heading south quick, don't just ignore it! Putting your head in the sand isn't going to fix anything here. You need to tactfully address the situation. You have a perspective. You have a gut feeling. Now, you need to check in with the other person to see if your assumptions are correct or if you've misunderstood what's going on.

Call me old fashioned, but this is why I hate people texting long conversations. There's NO context. You don't know if someone's comment was sarcastic, teasing, meant to be funny or downright rude. Instead, you'll make your assumption and run with it. If you're not sure - ASK!

How Do I Get Peace of Mind in Relationships Tip #3:

Let them know what you need. If someone has hurt your feelings, how do you want that interaction to change? What do you need instead? Can your needs be met by this person, or do you need to be meeting them, yourself, first?

A perfect example is the trap that we women tend to put our guys into when we ask them if some item of clothing looks good on us? Rarely are we wanting an honest answer.

We're "fishing" for a compliment and reinforcement that they find us attractive because we're doubting ourselves. First, you need to meet that need yourself. If you don't feel attractive, then what can you do to feel better about yourself. If you need more reinforcement, then flat out let them know, don't "fish."

Now, I know - not everyone is going to positively respond to these 3 techniques if you try to use them. Some people are going to get defensive. In those situations, you need to honestly look at what types of boundaries may need to be set around those relationships to keep them balanced and healthy for you.

Be sure to check back in, as I'll be discussing more in depth aspects of developing more meaningful relationships all this month. I want to help you feel confident in answering that daunting question of "How do I get peace of mind in relationships?"

Here are some helpful questions to think about - Which of these 3 steps is the most difficult for you? Why do you think that is? Be sure to answer those below in the comments section.

CHAPTER 9

SECRETS FOR SUCCESSFUL RELATIONSHIPS

Most of us encounter them everyday, whether at home, at work, or in the hours in between. They are so vital to our well-being yet relationships can also be the most challenging aspects of our lives. Whether casual, professional or personal, relationships define our lives and can be sources of tremendous pleasure and pain. How to navigate through relationships has become the focus of much discussion and investigation, especially in an age when technology can offers multiple attractive avenues for having relationships without leaving the comfort of your home. In this article I will highlight seven major characteristics of those who have highly successful relationships. This information has been gathered over the course of my studies and work as a physician specializing in interpersonal dynamics, human behavior, and emotional disorders.

#1. Make Agreements

In all relationships each person brings with them their own preferences, opinions, and methods of communicating. These personal traits may or may not match with those of the other, which can then lead to potential conflicts if one is not willing to compromise or even sacrifice some of their beliefs. People who have highly effective personal and professional relationships make agreements instead of engaging in conflicts. If someone is late in fulfilling some kind of obligation, there is an agreement in place about how to communicate about this. Of course you cannot anticipate every situation or circumstance and have an agreement set forth. What you can do is after a conflict has arisen, you can reflect back with the other person, recognize what went wrong in the communication, and then agree to do something better next time.

When someone disagrees with you, or has a different communication style, strong emotional reactions are often elicited that are hardwired into us from past experiences. By using agreements you are making a choice to change your style because it is likely the old pattern led to some undesirable outcome.

Essentially, you must be willing to take a critical look at your emotions, how you respond and be motivated for change. If you want your relationships to be effective, understand what you are contributing and how you can improve. If you leave someone else in charge of changing things for you, you will be disappointed with the results.

#2. They Don't Need Relationships

Let me repeat this one for clarity and emphasis. People who have successful relationships do not need the relationship, they want the relationship. They are not looking for the other person to fill some void in their life that has previously gone unfulfilled. Successful people take the time to understand themselves, are happy being alone and with another person, yet they seek out relationships and connections with others because they recognize the inherent value of interpersonal interactions. They go into the relationship with an open mind and ready for whatever comes their way.

Entering into a relationship searching for something, a characteristic of this person that was not present in the last, ultimately places some portion of your happiness dependent upon them. Placing someone else responsible for your emotions and feelings is a setup for disappointment. Learn how to be happy with yourself. Work on those parts of you that need improvement and when in any relationship, take full responsibility for your own happiness.

#3. Do Not Fall In Love With Someone's Potential

In personal relationships, we often see qualities in someone, perhaps just glimpses of them, that are endearing or attractive. These qualities may not be consistent or expressed enough to our liking, however, and you are left wondering about what the other could be like if he or she just acted that way all the time. "The relationship would be so much better, more exciting, more fulfilling," you might say to yourself. Our minds project forward into a future where all the positive characteristics of the other are constantly exhibited and you may think that person has so much potential.

Recognizing the potential is a definite positive. When it is the reason you are staying in the relationship, it is a negative. The person you see in the future is not the person you are with now and there is no way to predict if this person will evolve into the future one you envision.

Work on appreciating and understanding the person you are with in this moment because that is who they are and who they may always be. If you are not happy with the present person, you have a decision to make. Do you stay and accept this is who they may always be, or do you break it off and open yourself up to the possibility of something better?

Those who have successful relationships may have the ideal future partner in mind, but their focus is on the present.

#4. You Would Rather Be Happy Than Right

A majority of the arguments in personal and professional relationships are due to differences in opinion. You have a belief that differs from the other person's and you attempt to convince the other you are right, or vice versa. Depending on how hard one holds their opinions to be true determines how long the discussion or argument will persist. Worst case scenario, and one that occurs frequently, is that the conflict ends unresolved and the dispute is carried over to a future time.

A key to having functional relationships is placing your desire to be happy above your need to be right. It does not matter if you believe the other person is wrong and it is not your responsibility to prove it to them. Nor is it your place to fight for what you think is right. As a very astute philosopher once stated, "You have no rights. Having rights gives someone else the ability to wrong you."

Do not give someone else the power over your happiness. Place your happiness above all else, dismiss your need to be right, and chose to be happy instead. You will then find conflicts will decrease and the door then opens for improved communication.

#5. Know What Makes You Feel Loved AND Tell Them

This secret refers more to romantic relationships, though it is applicable to professional ones by the substitution of the word 'respected' for 'loved. How does someone know what makes you feel loved? The answer is simple. You must first understand what elicits that emotion and then tell the one you are with. This sounds like an easy process, yet few couples actually engage in this practice and miscommunication around this brings conflict with it.

As an example, let's say your partner experiences love as Chocolate. However, your understanding is your partner experiences love as Vanilla. Therefore, you go out and purchase vanilla ice cream, thinking you are demonstrating your love. The other becomes frustrated with you and says, "I just want you to love me!" Statements such as that bring strong emotions from the other person as they believed they were proving their love through Vanilla. What the partner really wanted was Chocolate and may find Vanilla offensive.

In all relationships, arguments ensue when one person feels unheard and the other believes they are not appreciated for their efforts. If one has a stronger desire to prove their point, to be right, the discord can escalate. To avoid this, declare what makes you feel loved, respected and appreciated, and then repeat this often. Do not assume your partner will remember. The more you reinforce it, the more likely it will be understood and acted upon.

#6. Be Honest

This secret is the most basic and leads to the most conflict when not followed. We all want and expect people to be honest with us, speak their true thoughts, desires and emotions. Furthermore, in relationships of any type, honesty is paramount to having trust in the other. Logically, what you expect from your partner you must give as well. You must be honest with someone if you expect honesty in return.

What frustrates most people in relationship situations is the doubt they have or the mistrust about the motives of their partner. People are experts at making assumptions, often negative ones, about the reasons behind someone's actions. If your partner says he/she will be home at 5pm, and they are not home by 6pm what does your mind think? What assumptions do you make about why the other is late, the type of person he/she is, or, what this action now means for the future?

Realistically, you have no way of knowing if your assumptions, logical or irrational, are true unless your partner tells you. Do not get stuck in assumptions. Focus on controlling what you can, yourself. Be honest in all situations, expect that in return, and point it out when you do not receive it. Be consistent in this practice and others will be honest in return.

As a physician, people frequently admit they were initially dishonest about their symptoms or lifestyle practices after they have had several visits. The reasons are many, such as fear and embarrassment, yet the majority of people admit their dishonesty when they feel they can trust me and I am honest with them. This holds true for all relationships.

Follow these guidelines, work on improving yourself, and successful relationships will be in your life.

CHAPTER 10

MAKING A RELATIONSHIP WORK

It's said, "A family that prays together stays together." There's probably more truth in that statement than meets the eye. Family cohesiveness needs glue to hold it together. Whether it's prayer or another form of communication, the recipe for a mindfulness relationship resides in taking responsibility.

When two people decide to have a relationship, each person must take 100% responsibility to make the relationship work. When one person slips below taking full responsibility, problems occur. Simply stated, both parties do for their relationship the things they know will enhance the relationship, not harm it.

Whether the relationship is with a friend or a lover, watch what happens when the relationship is working and when it is not. Anything less than taking 100% responsibility for making the relationship work cheats the relationship and throws it off-balance. One person is happy, and the other is not. When both parties take full responsibility, the relationship hums like a fine-tuned motor, and it runs smoothly. In a mindfulness relationship, people communicate a sense of contentment and happiness.

When each person takes 100% responsibility to make a relationship work, it works (period). That does not mean each person takes full responsibility for making the other person happy. Happiness is each person's responsibility, not his/her partner's. How often do you hear a man or woman say, "I did everything I possibly could to make my wife/husband happy, and nothing I did was ever enough!" Happiness comes from within, and it's not something someone can give.

Respect and admiration are things a person can give in a mindfulness relationship. They are ingredients to ensure a feeling of happiness because people enjoy being respected and admired. Interestingly enough, taking full responsibility for communicating respect for a partner is a reflection on how much a person respects their self. A person with little respect for their self can hardly be expected to communicate respect for a partner. So, in a relationship if you find a lack of respect from a partner, it's probably because the partner lacks respect for their self.

The same example can be applied to communicating admiration and taking responsibility for admiring a partner in a relationship. In other words, a person can love, admire and respect another as much as he/she loves, admires and respects their self.

The elusiveness of love is a never-ending chase. It's evident by the divorce statistics in America for marriage. According to DivorceStatistics.org, for first marriages - 45% to 50% of first marriages end in divorce. Second marriages - 60% to 67% of second marriages end in divorce. Third marriages - 70% - 73% of third marriages end in divorce. Couples with children divorce at about a 40% rate vs. couples without children divorce at about a rate of 66%.

People get married and divorced everyday. It's obvious by the divorce rate, and the innovative concept of mindfulness divorce being introduced by cutting-edge lawyers.

Mindfulness divorce is a fairly new concept. According to Thurman Arnold III, and taken from his website, ThurmanArnold.com:

"Mindfulness allows perspective based upon the Truth of our experience, not some trance-talking story about it all. For purposes of divorce, mindfulness begins by recognizing what is mindlessness and the forms of thinking and behavior that mindlessness takes. Mindfulness is being present at any given moment, in a conscious way.... Ultimately it is a practice and a commitment borne of desire, love and patience. "

At the beginning of a new relationship or bringing closure to a mature relationship, stick to the truth because it's the special few who take responsibility and enjoy the pleasure of a mindfulness family experience.

CHAPTER 11

MINDFULNESS MEDITATION THERAPY FOR EFFECTIVE STRESS MANAGEMENT

Emotional stress is something that we all experience when we have to cope with the many demands and responsibilities of home and work. Stress can be defined as an intense emotional and physiological reaction to a situation or the mental representation of a situation as a memory or anticipation. Chronic stress is produced when stress reactions do not resolve themselves and become habitual. The sustained physiological effects of chronic stress can have a serious effect on the body and lead to an increased risk of disease. The psychological effects of chronic stress produce fatigue, poor concentration and an impaired ability to perform tasks, which leads to more stress. Stress produces a general feeling of helplessness and negativity, both of which reinforce the stress reactions. We feel a lack of vitality, enthusiasm and creativity.

Many people describe chronic stress as a heavy blackness that covers everything.

Chronic stress can result in an increased chance of accidents as well as reducing work performance. Chronic stress also reduces our listening and learning skills and this reduces the quality of communication in our personal relationships and family. Chronic stress is a problem that greatly impacts those around us as well as reducing the quality of our own life.

It is well recognized that stress reactions are learned and originate from the influence of our own mental outlook and from belief patterns acquired from our parents, family and culture. Stress always contains both an objective component and a subjective component and in most situations it is the habitual subjective emotional reactivity that generates the emotional tension and physiological changes of stress. There is pain and there is suffering. Pain is the objective component that is often inevitable or unavoidable, but suffering is a subjective reaction that we generate and add to the pain. The Buddha described this subjective suffering as dukkha and not surprisingly, mindfulness, which is one of the main teachings of the Buddha, was and continues to be very relevant for working with and resolving emotional stress.

WORKING WITH STRESS REACTIONS

All habitual emotional reactions rely on two elements - ignorance and emotional energy. The first task in MMT is called RECOGNITION, in which we learn to recognize our stress reactions as they arise in stressful situations. This counteracts the automatic and mechanical part of what makes a reaction habitual. The maxim of MMT is that all change begins with mindfulness and awareness is the first and most important step. However, what keeps a reaction alive is the associated emotional charge without which the reaction would have no power to cause stress. MMT teaches us how to form a non-reactive relationship, the Mindfulness Based Relationship, with this underlying emotional energy that compels us to react.

The mindfulness relationship is very important. This is where we allow ourselves to open our awareness and investigate the emotional energy, which is quite different to our usual reaction of ignorance, avoidance or aversion.

Mindfulness creates a therapeutic space that allows the emotion to unfold and undergo transformation. If you give it space it will change. This is one of the great discoveries made by the Buddha, 2500 years ago and which we are rediscovering today. It is not what we do that matters as much as how we relate to our emotional stress. When this relationship is based on the receptivity and openness of mindfulness, then we create the best possible conditions in which the emotional tension can resolve itself. Without this emotional power, there is nothing to sustain the reaction and life-long patterns of stress producing reactivity begin to dissolve, leaving you free from their compulsive grip. Like the petals of a lotus bud that were previously held and constrained so tightly, the mind begins to explore a new freedom with all its possibilities and choices. This is the freedom that the Buddha talked about and that is possible for all of us to discover through the practice of mindfulness. MMT teaches you how to apply mindfulness to resolve your patterns of habitual reactivity so that you can realize your full potential and enjoy your life and relationships to the full.

CHAPTER 12

<u>MINDFULNESS PSYCHOTHERAPY FOR OVERCOMING ANXIETY AND FEAR</u>

Anxiety and depression affect most of us at some time in our lives. For many, and estimates vary from 10-50%, these powerful emotions can take hold and reduce our happiness and vitality, leaving us feeling fatigued and fearful. We become the victims of these emotions.

All emotions are created around a complex network of negative beliefs and negative patterns of thinking that we acquire over the years that become the prison bars that keep us penned up and suffering. The first part of making a change for the better is learning to recognize these negative patterns of habitual reactivity. Most of the time we aren't aware of these reactions when they arise - we just react out of habit. We tend to blindly accept the reactions as inevitable, the way things are. This provides our first challenge, right here. We have to break out of this delusion and understand that we are not the thoughts and emotions that arise in the mind; they are simply mind objects that arise due to conditions. Therefore, the first step in developing the art of recognizing our reactivity is to look at the reactions, emotions, worries and other negative thoughts as objects. We need to learn to look at these internal mental objects the same way that we might look at a table, a chair, a picture, or any other external object around us.

In fact, this is the first step in cultivating mindfulness meditation that we can practice right now. Settle into your chair, take a moment to relax your body and mind and start observing the objects around you. Pick an object and examine its details. Note how you can observe the object as it is: it exists in its space, and you exist as the observer, observing that object. You don't have to react to the object, and the object has no power over you. In other words you have a very spacious and open relationship with the object, without any overlay of reactivity. This is the nature of mindfulness and with careful practice you can develop this same kind of mindful relationship with your thoughts and emotions.

This is where mindfulness becomes an invaluable tool for both the client and the therapist. Mindfulness is defined as the non-reactive present-centered awareness of an experience. It is the art of sensitive listening, being fully present and receptive to whatever is being experienced. In Mindfulness Meditation Therapy, mindfulness is applied directly to the felt-sense of the emotion to cultivate this quality of presence. We choose to make the emotion the primary object of our meditation and our task is to develop a relationship with the emotion, with the anger or fear in which we can observe the emotion and allow the emotion to unfold. The purpose of cultivating the mindfulness-based relationship is so that we can move from the superficial surface structure of the emotion to the deep internal structure and reveal the subtle internal structure.

As we all know, it is what we don't see that has the greatest power over us, and this is exactly what happens with anxiety, depression and post-traumatic stress and anxiety. Through the mindfulness-based relationship that we cultivate with our inner emotional pain, we effectively allow it to change and witnessing this change is the essential part of the transformational process.

CHAPTER 13

Dating & Relationship Advice

Let's face it, sometimes we just don't think a relationship is going anywhere, and it's time to end things with the other person. Searching for dating & relationship advice at this point is just natural because you want to let the other person down as gently as possible. Below is some dating relationship advice that will help you let them down easy.

I strongly believe that all break ups should be done face to face if possible. This is much more personal than simply sending a break up letter, email, phone call, or text message (that one is the worst!). Set up a time where you can talk to the person face to face, one on one, with nobody else around to disrupt or listen in on you.

Let them know how you feel, and tell them the truth about why you are breaking up with them. A simple "it's not you, it's me" just doesn't cut it in most relationships, so make sure you search your soul to find the reason you are wanting to end the relationship. Maybe it's just that you have nothing in common or that you dislike something about their recent behavior. Whatever it is, tell them the truth.

Give them a chance to speak too. Listen to what they have to say and who knows, they might change your mind! Relationships are about giving and taking, so make sure that both of these happen for you when it comes to ending your relationship.

By following this dating & relationships advice, you will make the break up as easy as possible on both you and your soon to be ex boyfriend or girlfriend. Whatever you do, keep things brief. Don't keep stringing them along after you have already made up your mind, as this is just not fair.

CHAPTER 14

POWERFUL SOLUTIONS FOR RELATIONSHIP PROBLEMS

There is new hope in the challenge of creating the ideal relationship, or fixing a relationship in crisis.

What makes your relationships succeed or fail? Why do 60% of relationships fail and break up, and another 30% are well below satisfaction level for at least one of the couple? And why do we get into such relationships with apparently so little thought or planning? Well the answer is actually frighteningly simple. It is your unconscious programs that drive you into relationships, and it does so on the basis of false or unsubstantiated beliefs. But unless you do something about that you will continue to create the same behaviours and make the same decisions and mistakes.

Your unconscious mind is programmed with its formative beliefs before the age of five years old, when your mind is a sponge and you have no ability to evaluate what you are being told or what you see. In those years we take on the opinions and behaviours of those in authority over us, typically out parents. Our unconscious mind develops all our primary beliefs and values in that time and they then form the basis of most of our behaviours.

This is important in relationships because your unconscious programs determine who you are attracted to. Your values drive your behaviours and attitudes automatically, so unless you are actually aware of that and intervene in the process you will end up in the relationships that your unconscious program believes are what relationships are about. Because it is your parents relationship that is the basis of your belief system, the chance you will duplicate their relationship is very high. That may be a frightening thought for you if your parents did not have a great relationship!

To create a great relationship it is critical that you and your partner have at least 80% of common values, plus a significant level of tolerance or acceptance of those belief and values that you don't share. Anything less than this creates high levels of anxiety and irritation. The lower the values commonality the less likely the relationship will survive.

But there is hope. We now understand the processes of belief and values programming. Thirty five years of clinical work in understand the design and working of the mind has shown us the way of modifying how values and beliefs are processed. The natural progression of this is that you can design a relationship and find a partner who already shares a high level of real common values.

On the other hand, if you are already in a relationship, and both of you are open to the process, it is now possible to actually reprogram beliefs and values in a way that unconscious processes become automatic and congruent. This means that with some minor tweaking of the unconscious programs you can now fix relationships that are not working very well.

Certainly many relationships are initially driven by that wonderful sexual attraction. But sexual attraction alone is not enough to create a long-term relationship, and frankly many relationships can not be fixed. But if you start with a minimum of 40-50%

common values, any relationship can be fixed.

If you don't currently have a long-term stable relationship, think about the possibility of creating the perfect relationship - perhaps even the elusive "soul" relationship. Makes your heart jump does it not?

CHAPTER 15

CONSCIOUS ATTENTION TO WHAT MATTERS

The world is demanding and constantly changing. People tend to ignore one of their most important anchors for intellectual sanity, emotional security, and spiritual wisdom-their primary relationship with a mate. A committed, lifelong relationship with another human being is a simple, obvious, and profound source of happiness, but relationships ring in low on many couples' list of priorities. Although people might say their relationship is very important, their actual behavior contradicts them. Individuals become preoccupied with worldly matters (careers, material goods, social position) and begin to take their partners for granted. When attention goes elsewhere, the relationship anchor cuts loose and the relationship drifts out to sea.

This situation does not just happen to you. You are not the helpless victim of a world characterized by the popular, albeit misinformed, saying "Life is hard and then you die." In fact, you are a co-creator of your situation and you can just as easily create something different and new using the power of Mind Freedom.

How To Think About Your Relationship

Your relationship success flows from paying sustained attention to your relationship. How you think about your relationship is typically dictated by learned beliefs and assumptions, many of which are negative and can lead you from one relationship failure to another. Become aware of relationship-negative messages you give yourself and others, and then intentionally shift them to positive messages. Here are two examples:

1. Having time for each other. Want more time with your partner?

Focus on your desire to be together. Picture the moments you've had together and the pleasure that brings. If other thoughts begin to whiningly intrude ("But we have so much to do. We can't take time even though I want to. Other things are more pressing.") let them pass through.

Replace them with: "We do have a lot going on in our lives, but we're important and I want more time together. I know we can find some way to make that happen." Possibilities will present themselves; situations will arise when you can choose to spend time together or not. Seize those opportunities.

2. Sustainability of Relationships. Want to spend a lifetime with your mate?

Picture the two of you growing happy and healthy together into old age. When learned assumptions insinuate themselves into your head ("Most relationships don't last," "Passion dies," "Lovers grow apart.") send them out the window.

Replace them with: "Our relationship will thrive throughout the years." Act on every opportunity that emerges to intensify your connection.

CHAPTER 16

MINDFULLY APPRECIATING YOUR PARTNER

Practicing gratitude may be the fastest single pathway to relationship happiness and success.

According to a study conducted by positive psychologist and mindfulness expert, Dr. Henry Emmons, PhD, people who kept a gratitude journal for just 3 weeks measured 25% higher on life satisfaction after wards. Research participants who became more mindful of gratitude, exercised more, drank alcohol less, and were describe by their families and friends as generally nicer to be around.

Developing a habit of noticing what you appreciate about your partner can be a very powerful "dumb fight" prevention tool.

Conflict in a relationship is normal and to be expected. As one famous marriage counselor said, "When choosing a long-term partner, you will inevitably be choosing a particular set of unsolvable problems that you'll be grappling with for the next ten, twenty or fifty years."

Happy couples and unhappy couples can fight the same amount. However, the couples that stay together have better "repair moves" because of what is called "positive sentiment override," a term coined by John Gottman, PhD. Relationship success actually depends on the ratio of positive to "disappointing." Couples can have quite a lot of conflict and still be close if the ratio of positive interactions to negative interactions is at least 5 to 1. Positive interactions come from understanding, accepting, and supporting one another.

Appreciation is feels good to your partner but it is also going to make YOU feel great. Being mindful of what you like, value, and appreciate will help you:

• become less judgmental

• increase your satisfaction

• increase flexibility and acceptance

• let go of gripes

• deepen your trust

• soften you and make you more kind

• increase your motivation to be generous

• make you more empathic

A good relationship is not something that "happens," it is something that you must deliberately create. So every day, make it a practice of noticing at least three things you appreciate about your partner. You can actually keep a journal and make daily notes. The qualities don't have to be huge; they can be tiny. It might be the way a look, a tone of voice, a touch.

If you find yourself having more than your fair share of dumb fights with your partner, it is good to remember what qualities attracted you to your partner in the beginning of the relationship. Do you remember the personal qualities that you most admired about him/ her? In all likelihood, those strengths and qualities are still there today, you just have to pay attention.

CHAPTER 17

<u>MINDFULNESS AND INTIMATE RELATIONSHIPS</u>

Mindfulness means: you pay attention to and are aware of whatever happens within you regarding your life and relationships.

When you practice mindfulness you become empowered to develop a successful and healthy intimacy. The reason being, that the more you pay attention the more aware you become of yourself (your needs, fears, expectations, fantasies, reactions and behaviors); and as you become aware of yourself the more empowered you become to make conscious decisions regarding your life and relationships (whether you currently have a relationship or attempt to develop one).

Four layers of a mindfulness intimacy are:

1. Paying attention, which enables you to stop acting on automatic pilot. As you pay attention you become able to act with full

awareness, making appropriate decisions regarding situations you encounter in your life and in your relationships (either with your current partner, or with a new partner). When you pay attention, notice and become aware of what there is, you can then decide what changes you would like to make.

2. Observation: Paying attention is based on observation: you observe yourself, your thoughts, attitudes and emotions, reactions and behaviors.

3. Acceptance: when you observe, with full mindfulness and pay attention to what is, it is crucial that you accept what you notice. Acceptance is vital, since as long as you don't accept what there is you can't make a change, because you deny what there is and therefore don't see a need for a change.

4. Making a change: Change is possible when you accept what you observe. Denying and rejecting what you see don't lead you to personal growth (and to living life and relationships to the fullest, since you don't accept parts of yourself which are, after all, part of "who you are", parts which often lead you to harm your relationships).

When you observe, pay attention and accept, you can then make a change. The reason being, that you become free to make conscious decisions, rather than continue acting on automatic pilot (like you might have acted until now). Being free you can contemplate new ways of behavior (rather than behaving, once again, according to your old harmful patterns), choosing a behavior which you think/feel best suits you and the current situation, whether with your current partner or in a new relationship.

Be careful not to be your own worst enemy

There are those whom the process of mindfulness might scare them, who might prefer to go on with things as they are rather than look inwards and make changes. I you are among them, you might deny and reject, rather than accept what you observe. You will then convince yourself that you don't have such and such attitudes, behaviors and/or characteristics; that you are not responsible for whatever it is that goes wrong with your relationship. You will also convince yourself that you know yourself well enough and that there is nothing you need to explore and learn about yourself.

Such self-conviction might misguide you: it will "persuade" you that you are o.k. (and your partner not); that you know yourself well enough (even if you don't); that there is nothing for you to change (even if there is).

If you take the "easy route" - accepting these convictions rather than beginning with the process of mindfulness: paying attention, observing, becoming aware and accepting what you see - you sabotage yourself, by not enabling yourself see things you need to see (about yourself, your partner and your relationship) and making the decisions you need to make in order to finally become empowered to develop a successful, healthy and satisfying intimate relationship.

How to benefit from the process of mindfulness

When you get up the courage and the motivation to go through the process of mindfulness, observe, pay attention, become aware and accept what you see, the more self-understanding and personal-growth you gain, and the more empowered you become to develop a successful intimate relationship.

142

CHAPTER 18

MINDFULNESS MEDITATION THERAPY FOR SUCCESSFUL RELATIONSHIP

MMT is an exciting new development in which mindfulness is applied directly to help transform and resolve difficult emotional states such as anxiety, fear, phobias, anger and other forms of habitual emotional reactivity that affects the quality of our happiness and the quality of our personal relationships.

Personal relationships provide one of the greatest challenges in life and most of us will experience difficulties with patterns of habitual reactivity triggered by our partner, our children or other family members. Our buttons get pushed and we become angry or upset, fearful or anxious. This dynamic is based on learned habitual reactivity and both the perpetrator and victim are compelled to react, often against their better judgment. You may say something knowing that it will cause offense, but are unable to stop yourself from saying it. The victim also feels compelled to react by taking offense and becoming upset or angry. These reactive dynamics take away our freedom and erode the delicate and fragile nature of all relationships, making it hard to feel love and compassion, leaving us bitter and contracted with a closed heart.

However, what has been learned through conditioning can be unlearned through mindfulness. The key to changing these repetitive patterns of habitual reactivity in both the victim and perpetrator is to first learn, through practice, to recognize reactivity in all its forms as it arises. Reactivity depends and thrives on two principle factors: ignorance and emotional charge. Ignorance, or the unawareness of reactivity causes us to repeat the reaction over and over again, like a machine. The first phase of MMT is primarily about learning to recognize reactions as and when they arise and replace ignorance with awareness. This is the first function of mindfulness, the factor of RECOGNITION. Without this most basic first step nothing can change, but with awareness comes the possibility of change. Recognition is the beginning of the transformational process and often this skill alone is sufficient to totally change the whole reactive dynamic between two people.

The next phase of MMT involves changing how we view the reaction and associated emotional energy. This is called REFRAMING and is one of a number of skills that is taught in the psychological science of Neuro-Linguistic Programming (NLP) and which is another chief modality used in MMT. Normally, (ie when we are unaware) we identify with emotional reactions and literally become the reaction. When a reaction of feeling hurt arises, we become the emotional reaction of hurting. Anger arises and we become angry. We say "I am upset," or "I am angry" because we literally take on the entire identity of the emotion. During reframing, we learn to stop this automatic process of subjective identification and learn to see the reaction as an object that is not self, but simply a phenomenon that has arisen in our consciousness due to various causes and conditions. When the reaction of feeling upset arises, we learn to see it as an object within us, rather like seeing a bubble rising in a pond. The bubble is not the pond, but simply a small object within the pond and the emotion is not our self, but simply a small part within our self. After reframing the emotion, we learn to say, "I notice a feeling of hurting within me" or "I notice anger arising in my mind." This is a very important step, because it counteracts the habitual tendency to react and opens up a sense of space and choices around the emotion.

The next phase of MMT, after RECOGNITION and REFRAMING is the most important step of forming a RELATIONSHIP with the internal felt-sense of the emotional reaction. Let us explore this in more detail. Once you have recognized a reaction and made it into an object that you can see and experience, then you begin to see the emotional reaction as an object to be investigated and known in its own right, rather than getting entangled in the storyline of who did what to whom or who is right and who is wrong. The storyline may be very compelling and you may feel very offended or hurt, but indulging in negative, emotionally charged thinking is seldom an effective tool for resolving emotional conflict. This is the first function of mindfulness - learning to recognize a reaction, seeing it as an object and not getting seduced into further reactivity.

The kind of relationship that we cultivate in MMT is called the Mindfulness Based Relationship. This relationship has certain unique qualities. The first and most important quality is non-reactivity. By learning to recognize reactivity, we can stop the tendency to proliferate further reactivity in the form of reactive thinking, or further emotional reactions of aversion and displeasure. The second characteristic of the mindfulness-based relationship is about opening our heart and mind and developing a quality of genuine caring towards the inner pain of our anger or resentment. Instead of turning away, we turn towards our suffering. This does not mean that we indulge in feeling sorry for ourselves and certainly does not mean that we indulge in reactive thinking. Rather, we learn to be fully present with our inner emotion with a keen level of attention. The third quality of mindfulness is investigation. We turn towards our pain, we become attentive and then we take this further step and investigate the deeper inner structure of the experience. What seemed like the solid emotion of anger or resentment begins to unfold into a complex interior landscape of subtle feelings and memories and very often, some form of experiential imagery.

This is the fourth phase of MMT: TRANSFORMATION and RESOLUTION. The exact nature of what unfolds is unique to each person, but the effect of becoming aware of this inner detailed structure is highly transformational. Often, beneath anger there is sadness and beneath resentment there is fear. These more subtle feelings may give rise to further feelings and experience. During the process of transformation, emotions literally dissolve into many small parts, which can be more readily digested and re-integrated by the psyche and our innate intelligence into something more stable. This is the final step of MMT, called RESOLUTION. Any form of emotional suffering, or dukkha, as it is called in Buddhism, represents a state of instability and conflict in the psyche. The psyche hates instability and will always try to resolve dukkha if given the freedom to change. Mindfulness provides the therapeutic space and freedom in which transformation and resolution can occur.

In this way, each person in the relationship works with his or her individual reactive habits. Each learns to identify reactions, develops a mindfulness-based relationship with the underlying felt-sense of each reaction and then allows the internal structure of the experience to unfold into finer detail leading to the transformation and resolution of the compulsive emotional energy that makes us react against our will. When there is freedom from reactivity, we begin to discover new possibilities, new choices in how we respond to the challenges of being in a relationship. The process may be more complex than is explained here, but the underlying theme is quite simple and it is about engaging with our experience, whether pleasant or painful with the faculty of mindfulness. If you can do this, then healing will proceed quite naturally.

CHAPTER 19

THE MINDFULNESS APPROACH

For a marriage or significant personal relationship to work, both parties must be willing and able to cultivate a level of communication that is highly receptive and responsive to the needs of the other person, and this communication needs to flow in both directions. Any blockage in this flow leads to misunderstanding and conflict. Real communication is highly dynamic and constantly changing and adjusting to changing needs. In the ideal relationship each person is sensitive to the other, not only listening to the words spoken but also sensing the body language being expressed, sensing the meaning communicated through voice tone, facial expression and posture. It is, therefore, no surprise that in order to be able to receive all this verbal and non-verbal information and in order to be able to respond in a sensitive manner, there must be an extraordinary degree of openness of both mind and heart. A closed mind can receive nothing and cannot respond appropriately to the needs of a given situation. Therefore, we must understand the processes that lead to the closing of the mind, and the processes that lead to the opening of the mind and heart, and we must understand both processes in depth if we are to develop and maintain good communication in our marriage or relationship.

The biggest problem that leads to the breakdown of a marriage or other significant relationship is when we become dominated by patterns of Habitual Emotional Reactivity. A reactive mind is a closed mind, unable to respond creatively and intelligently to the needs of the present moment. Compassion and sensitivity are absent, or greatly diminished, and we become little more than a machine, mechanically reacting to the other person.

We become locked into cycles of habitual reactivity. He says this, she feels that; she does this, he feels that. We become victims of this habitual emotional reactivity and compelled to react with frustration and disappointment, becoming easily upset and often reacting with anger as we feel misunderstood or unloved. Our inner reactive Self engages with the reactive Self of the other person in a repeating cycle of hurt and suffering. This process creates a wedge between us and drives us apart. When our relationship is dominated by reactivity then what we experience is loneliness and emptiness and great sadness.

So, in any relationship there are four entities engaging each other: The True Self of each person, which is not conditioned and not limited by habitual reactivity, tries to interact through the medium of openness, awareness and friendliness to the True Self of the other person. However, this is complicated by the relationship between the two Reactive Selves, based on conflict and duality. Not surprisingly, relationships can become quite messy!

When you were in love that is when the True Selves were communicating freely. But over time we lose that connection and bad habits become dominant; the Reactive Selves hold power, love is abandoned and the fighting takes over. The Reactive Self becomes hard and unyielding, aggressive and also very fearful. People can spend their whole marriage lost in this blind conflict between the Reactive Selves.

We need to learn how to let go of the Reactive Self and re-connect with our True

Self, which is the source of unconditional love, patience, kindness, gentleness and intuitive intelligence. This True Self is within us all the time - it just gets lost and covered over by the layers of reactive habits. With mindfulness at our side, we gradually lift off these hard layers that have imprisoned the True Self and we discover the joy of how to communicate again. We re-discover the passion and simple bliss of the love that we once shared. Now we have the tools to handle conflict and emotional pain; guilt and hurt; anger and remorse; in a completely different way - based on mindfulness and innate love.

CHAPTER 21

MIND CONTROL SKILLS FOR BETTER RELATIONSHIPS

1. Choose Your Outcomes Wisely

A man who is stressed is no lover. A woman who is needy, is no partner. A friend who is in crisis is no friend and parents who are always busy are not really doing their job.

It is so easy to let life dictate our destiny. A stressed husband will become single. A needy partner will become dejected. A friend in crisis will become an enemy and parents who are always busy will see their busY-ness waste another life.

To dictate your destiny exert your influence over your body. Make it your student, not your teacher.

By determining the best for your body you must determine what you want. If you want pleasure, then determine that this is your number 1 priority and please don't complain that you are fat, unhealthy or ugly. Pleasure has a downside, a balancing opposite called pain. All pain comes from the seeking of pleasure. So, if you want pleasure in the body, please accept the balance, pain.

However, if you want love and relationship then your body pleasure is not a priority. If your body pleasure is a priority in relationship then you are going to have short term pleasure long term pain.

If you want long term pleasure, then you need to accept short term pain and that pain is simply self-discipline. What goes into your body for pleasure causes pain. What goes into your body for the love of health and relationship and family causes only love and health. Do you eat for pleasure, or to deal with emotional pain like tiredness and depression, funk or hopelessness? If so, that remedy is going to take you to a regretful destiny. Short term pleasure relief, long term pain.

Determine your outcome, the destiny you want. If you want a loving and inspired relationship eat and drink to create it. If you want short term pleasure and instantaneous gratification, admit it, and eat for it. There's no right or wrong here, just consequence. (alcohol, sugar, coffee, dairy, pastry are all short term gratification foods, salt is the best one)

2. Remain Independent

In your relationships there are going to be disagreements in opinion and style. If there's any anxiety or emotion from such disagreements then it's wise to let it go. Two people in a relationship need disagreement. Agreement will be boring and uneventful.

If your partner takes offence at disagreements then learn to shut your words, but don't shut your brain. Your opinion is weighted with 50% of the accuracy of truth. So, simply try to add their opinion to your opinion and hold two opinions as valid instead of wanting either agreement or their compliance in your opinion.

Opinions are where we lose our independence. The more opinionated we are the less independent we are. Opinions are just ways the ego has to create identity. If my opinion of Whale Hunting is both a good and a bad thing then I have no identity from that opinion. If, of course, I become anti Whale Hunting, I form an opinion and that is the basis on which I build a false identity. "Anti Whale Hunting Person." This is Ego...and the loss of free independent thought, at its worst.

One can also lose independence in a relationship through opinions on religious beliefs, environmental beliefs and behavioural beliefs. Such things are poor frameworks for healthy love to live.

3. Fill Your Voids

Our mind is not as liberated as we think. It is conditioned to a certain range of thinking and therefore mind control becomes more simple when we know how our mind is going to work. Our mind seeks to fill our voids.

So, much love is not love at all. Instead, it's the filling of voids and the attraction that's associated with it.

Peter meets Mary. Two years ago, if Peter met Mary he wouldn't have blinked sideways. But now, suddenly Peter finds Mary attractive. Mary found Peter interesting two years ago, and nothing has changed. She's a little surprised. "What changed?" asks Mary.

What changed is Peter's voids. Two years ago Peter wasn't wanting babies. Two years ago Peter wanted money. Two years ago Mary didn't fill Peter's voids. Now, Peter wants babies and Mary is perfect.

Jane left Michael. But she keeps going back. While they are together Jane recognises that she's got unfulfilled needs, more voids than Michael can meet. So, when together Jane is discontent and anxious. However, when they part, Jane suddenly realises she has some voids that, while she was with Michael got filled. So, Jane is caught between a rock and a hard place, unfulfilled with Michael, unfulfilled without him. She yoyo's back and forward in her relationship and silly Michael, takes her back. Obviously Jane fills one of

Michael's voids too. The dance goes on till they both get sick of it, or sick from it.

The best way to take care of this is to know yourself. Know your voids and respect that relationships and your attraction to your partner are void filling. If ever you fill those voids for yourself, the attraction for that partner will die out.

Mind control in this sense is to be aware of the voids your partner fills in your life and always remember how important that person is to you. It's easy to become complacent and take someone for granted and then want to leave... better to stay humble and thankful.

4. Ignore Advice You Didn't Ask For

Your body is going to be either a student of yours, or your teacher, or both. There's no need for advice from the outside. Your body will tell you when you screw up, lose your mind, become emotionally overloaded or off track. And, as a good student it will respond well when what you eat, do and think are authentic.

All sorts of people give themselves permission to coach you. The worst of those is your partner. Love is learning to shut up. So, if your partner keeps advising you on matters you didn't ask for advice about, just know that the more you listen, the more you'll get and the more you listen and get, the less loved you are. People only try to change others in order to make it easier to love them.

CHAPTER 22

HOW TO GUIDE AND FREE MEDITATION

Here I explore a brief definition of the practice and it's Western Psychological benefits. At the end there is a Mindfulness Meditation Guide for your own personal practice.

Mindfulness plays a central role in the teaching of Buddhist meditation where it is affirmed that "correct" or "right" mindfulness is the critical factor in the path to liberation and subsequent enlightenment.

Described as "a calm awareness of one's body functions, feelings, content of consciousness, or consciousness itself, it is the seventh element of the Noble Eightfold Path, the practice of which supports analysis resulting in the development of wisdom." ~Wikipedia

The analysis that many Buddhist traditions hold as being the highest level knowledge is experiential experience. You essentially achieve wisdom of the intricacies and subtleties of yourself by simply observing your physical body, feelings and thoughts.

With this development of self-awareness you essentially fine tune yourself to engage more efficiently in your surroundings and develop the ability to return to a state of "presence", aiming to be in this present moment state perpetually.

This calm awareness also refines your attention in a very simple yet perfect way - simplicity almost always is the most effective - and in this case gently bringing your attention to scanning your body, observing your breath and acknowledging your thoughts, brings a refined attention to the outer dimension - engaging in business activities, sports, reading, relationships etc.

Mindfulness practice, inherited from the Buddhist tradition, is increasingly being employed in Western psychology to alleviate a variety of mental and physical conditions, including obsessive-compulsive disorder, anxiety, chronic pain and in the prevention of relapse in depression and drug addiction.

Dr. Jon Kabat-Zinn a Professor of Medicine Emeritus from the University of Massachusetts is the pioneer of this Western influx of meditation, with the flood of current studies and research from neuroscience, neuro-imaging, psychology and more we can now conclude that Meditation is the only effective mental health practice we have - not only to cure ailments but to increase memory and develop cognitive abilities.

Below is a Guide to enter a state of Mindfulness Meditation, and as with any technique that allows you to enter the Meditative State the most important element is to engage in regular practice, which will not only bring about the relaxation response but will develop Self-Awareness connecting more deeply to what you are doing, in creativity and intuition.

Be playful and be patient and most of all Enjoy the practice!

Awareness Meditation:

Mindfulness Meditation for Relaxation & Clarity

Take a couple of nice deep breaths

• In through nose out through mouth

• Breathing in chest expanding

• Breathing out relaxation releasing tension etc

• Repeat for a few moments

Now bring back to natural breath breathing in and out rhythmically.

Shift attention to the physical sensation of the weight of your body pressing on the chair.

• In particular the contact of the body on the chair beneath you.

• Notice if the weight falls down evenly through the body.

• Notice if you are leaning slightly to the left or the right.

In the same way notice the sensation on the soles your feet as well

• Where is the point of contact strongest? is it on the heel the toe inside or outside of the foot?

Again the hands and the arms just feeling the weight of your hands on your knees

This isn't an exercise trying to stop your thoughts

• Just allow them to come and go.

• The point is just to be aware of the exercise and if your thoughts drift you off just gently come back to the practice.

Also notice the sounds

• Often sounds seem like a distraction but they can heighten your exercise.

• Gauge the distance of each sound with no evaluation, no expectation.

As soon as you realize that your mind has wandered off, just gently bring attention back to your body

How does your body feel? Feeling of Relaxation, do you perhaps feel restless agitated?

• Don't change the way you feel, but I'd like to have you get a good sense about how you feel.

• Start at your toes and mentally scan from the toes up to the top of the head

• Just noticing which part of the body feels relaxed, comfortable, and which parts are tense or tight.

• Starting off from the toes - use specifics each toe, sole of foot, heel, ankle etc.

Don't worry if the mind wanders off that is fine, as soon as you realize just gently come back to the sensation

As you're doing this you might get a sense how you actually feel and what your mood is - we very rarely are not connected to this understanding

You might feel a rising falling sensation chest diaphragm stomach - take a few seconds to find out where you feel it in your body

• Assess the rhythm of your breath; is it short, fast, slow?

• Take a few seconds to assess - there is no right or wrong way of breathing.

• Be aware and mindful of how your body breaths naturally

• Now Shift to counting the rising and falling of your breaths.

• Count to 10 then stop and start back at 1.

If the mind wanders gently come back.

If your breathing is very faint then you can gently put hand on chest to observe the rise and fall of your breathing.

If the mind wanders gently come back.

It's not about controlling the mind it is about stepping back and allowing the thoughts to flow naturally.

Observing your breath

Remember don't try to control your breath just allow yourself to breath.

Just for a moment just let go of your focus for a few seconds, allow it be completely free, no effort required no sense of control - just allow your mind to be.

Very gently bring your attention back to the physical sensation of your body, feeling the weight of gravity, soles of feet on the floor, any sounds notice them.

In your own time when you are ready gently open your eyes again casting a lucid gaze just aware of the space around the room.

CHAPTER 23

HOW MINDFULNESS CAN HELP YOU REDUCE STRESS

The Scourge of Modern Life

Chances are, if you are reading this right now you have access to electricity, an internet connection and a smartphone.

You live in the industrialised world and have been affected by stress at some point in your life.

Stress in modern times is unavoidable.

It is the frontier for worry and anxiety, reflecting the conditions our ancestors faced on the plains of the Savannah centuries ago.

The mention of stress has found its way into everyday use, teenagers now use the term to describe rising stress levels studying for mid-term exams.

But are we stressed or feigning the symptoms to drawn attention to our struggles?

One thing is certain, stress is real. Yet how your body interprets it varies from person to person.

In fact, your tolerance for stress is different to a trained Navy Seal soldier. Yet, we can all agree, when pushed beyond our stress point, our health declines.

The good news is, we can use mindfulness to help us navigate the torrents of stress and manage our lives better.

Mindfulness means paying attention in a particular way; with purpose, in the present moment, and non-judgementally.

It helps you cope with life's challenges by being present and inhabiting your body with attentiveness. This is in contrast to runaway thoughts which pass through your mind without your conscious awareness.

"Mindfulness - the steady, non-judgmental awareness and acceptance of experience - leads to self-awareness and to shifts in our perspectives that allow us to see clearly what's happening and how we are reacting, to respond to triggers and traumas with far more open-mindedness, and to face the process of necessary change with far more flexibility and tolerance," affirm author Linda Graham MFT in, Bouncing Back: Rewiring Your Brain for Maximum Resilience and Well-Being.

Lurking Beneath Surface

Practising mindfulness can help you reduce stress because it shifts your autonomic nervous system from a stressed state to a calm state.

As you are reading this, there are minor stresses taking place in the background you are unaware of, yet your subconscious mind is attentive to.

Stress is insidious. It lurks beneath the surface and strikes when you least expect it, carrying with it accumulated stress from the past which can tip you over the edge.

I liken it to a sequinned pearl necklace, cut at one point and left to unravel into pieces. Stress has the same effect causing life to crumble if left untreated.

Mindfulness can help you cope with the habitual patterns of thinking that dominate your everyday life.

"The practice of mindfulness - training the brain to focus its attention and to strengthen conscious awareness - allows us to see our conditioned patterns of response clearly so that we can get unstuck from them when we need to," avows Linda Graham MFT.

Mindfulness helps you notice the stream of thoughts passing through your mind moment to moment.

It is a means to check in with yourself to notice what is taking place beneath the surface of your thoughts.

You may be prone to reacting to external conditions, yet seldom take the time to note your emotional well-being. It is often too late when you sense something because an emotional crisis has occurred.

Your thoughts can pull you into the past, where you re-experience uninviting events.

You are not present, but recalling a mental screenplay taken place long ago.

This becomes a stressor because you bring unresolved emotions into your interactions with others, contaminating the beauty of the present moment.

"But any time you let your thoughts, worries, and stresses dictate how you experience this moment, you inevitably suffer, because you're in conflict with reality, with truth. Rather than dancing with life, you're in a wrestling match-and the outcome of the struggle isn't in doubt," declares author Hugh G. Byrne in, The Here-and-Now Habit: How

Mindfulness Can Help You Break Unhealthy Habits Once and for All.

Carving Out Time for Silence

Mindfulness can go a long way when you devote regular time for silence.

This is attained through meditation and the sensations created in the body.

Meditation anchors your mind to the present moment, so you become attentive to your present moment experience.

It is important not to fight your thoughts or add a commentary to what you feel, but allow yourself to connect with your feelings.

As you become comfortable sitting in silence, you may wish to advanced your practice via structured meditation. This is ideal to strengthen your knowledge and take you into a deeper meditative state.

The benefits of meditation allow you to detach from your thoughts. You become a silent witness and less invested in the stream of activity created in the mind.

You are less reactive because you interact with what is taking place before you.

Stress abounds because people believe their thoughts.

So, if you are driving home after a hostile encounter with your boss or colleague, and an inconsiderate motorist cuts you off in traffic, you offer them a piece of your mind.

Yet, by practising mindfulness you become attuned to the physical sensations of anger before you retaliate since you are mindful of your emotional state.

Linda Graham MFT affirms, "Mindful awareness - observing and reflecting - allows us to step back from the experience of the moment and observe it from a larger field of awareness that is not any of those experiences, that is larger than any of those patterns. With that awareness, we can begin to see different possibilities for responding."

Mindfulness has a positive effect on your relationships. Your emotional well-being is enriched, instead of succumbing to external stimuli.

The success of mindfulness-based stress reduction lies in noting your thoughts non-judgmentally, through the eyes of equanimity and compassion.

In doing so, you recognise thoughts pass through the landscape of your mind and they needn't turn into negative emotions.

We are heavily invested in our thoughts and have a negativity bias when challenged. This is an evolutionary mechanism to help us make sense of our environment.

So, when thoughts, feelings or sensations emerge, don't ignore them or suppress them, nor analyse or judge them.

Note them as they occur and observe them intentionally but non-judgmentally, moment by moment, in your field of awareness.

If your mind wanders say to yourself, "wandering" and bring your mind back to the present moment.

If you wish to be happy and live a peaceful life, be mindful of your thoughts before they lead you down a perilous path.

Stressful thoughts are not the source of your happiness, but a by-product of unconscious thinking left to run wild.

Mindfulness helps you to reduce stress because it anchors you to the present moment where your body inhabits.

After all, if your body is present doesn't it make sense that your mind also be here and now?

CHAPTER 24

STUDY FINDS MINDFULNESS MEDITATION REDUCES LONELINESS

Loneliness is a widespread problem in Western society, especially among older adults, which doesn't seem to get enough attention. As adults grow older, there is a tendency for them to become more isolated from their families and society in general.

A study published recently in a scientific journal found that mindfulness meditation helps older adults overcome loneliness. This is good news for seniors because loneliness is a major risk factor for various health conditions such as Alzheimer's and cardiovascular disease.

Growing Old, and Lonely

Before we go on, it's important to understand that loneliness is more of a feeling of social disconnection, rather than a physical isolation. There are various reasons why older adults can experience more loneliness. Here are just a few:

• Empty nest syndrome - Parents who have been busy caring for their children suddenly find themselves with much more free time after the kids leave the house.

• Rusty social skills - After so many years of being busy raising children, many parents have not been practicing their social skills with people their age.

• Set in our ways - Most of us know that we tend to become set in our ways as we get older. This means that we take fewer risks in trying new things, which is exactly what meeting new people is all about.

• Lack of social networks - In addition to having rusty social skills, parents have not been active developing their own social networks.

• Increase in children's family responsibilities - As older adults reach retirement age, their children are often at the height of their careers and family responsibilities. So, they have less time for their aging parents.

To make matters worse, studies have shown that loneliness is contagious. Lonely people tend to spread loneliness by pushing other people away, instead of engaging them. This is probably because of the fear of rejection. Lonely people are generally more fearful, so meeting new people involves greater risk from their perspective.

Social Networking Programs Have Limited Success

Studies have shown that social networking programs for older adults have not been very effective. The reason is that they approach the problem from the outside, when loneliness is primarily an internal mental condition.

In addition, most social networking programs don't help people develop core social skills such as deep listening, mindful speech, compassion, and forgiveness. They simply put people together in social settings and expect them to interact and develop meaningful relationships.

In order for social networking programs to be more effective, they would need to address both the internal and external factors that lead to loneliness. In other words, they would need to teach people social skills, and then help them develop their networks.

How Mindfulness Meditation Helps Overcome Loneliness

It is not surprising that the recent study by professor J. David Creswell, Director of the Health and Human Performance Laboratory at Carnegie Mellon University, found that mindfulness meditation helps older adults overcome loneliness. This is because the practice addresses the main source of the problem-the human psyche. One thing that mindfulness meditation does is help us see our interconnectedness with the rest of humanity.

The main benefit of mindfulness meditation is that it helps people live in the present moment. This is particularly important to overcoming loneliness because the internal and external causes of loneliness take place in the present moment-that is, our emotions and interactions with other people.

The practice also helps them develop more effective social skills. For those who practice mindfulness meditation regularly, loneliness diminishes significantly because they can cultivate more intimate and meaningful relationships with people without fear of rejection. Practitioners learn to practice deep listening, mindful speech, compassion, forgiveness, and other relevant social skills.

In essence, mindfulness meditation addresses both the internal and external factors that lead to loneliness.

Living Rich and Fulfilling Lives

There are several health benefits from overcoming loneliness-both physical and psychological. The physical benefits include lower risk of Alzheimer's and heart disease. Dr. Creswell's study also indicated that people who practice mindfulness meditation may live longer.

Researchers measured the inflammatory response of the body, and found that those who meditated had a lower level of C-reactive protein (CRP), which is a marker commonly used in measuring inflammation. Elevated levels of CRP have been associated with higher risk of inflammatory disease and death.

The greatest psychological benefit of overcoming loneliness is a greater sense of belonging. People who are not lonely live rich and fulfilling lives. Once their children leave the house and become preoccupied with their own lives, parents are able to develop their own social networks and enjoy their new lives without the daily pressures of raising children. In general, they are much happier.

From a societal perspective, we can also argue that mindfulness meditation will help reduce the strain on Medicare. If the practice can reduce loneliness and its related health consequences, then it can reduce the associated costs to the individuals on fixed incomes, the Medicare system, and the taxpayers.

Getting Started in Your Practice

Studies like the one cited above continue to confirm what many mindfulness meditation practitioners already suspected. We owe a debt of gratitude to researchers like Dr. Creswell and his team. Their studies are not only helping build the credibility of mindfulness meditation, but they are also helping achieve greater awareness of the practice and its benefits to all areas of our lives.

Now that we know that mindfulness meditation can help us overcome loneliness, it's time to put that knowledge into practice. What I recommend to beginners is that they learn the basics of the practice and meditate for about 20 to 30 minutes daily. I also recommend about 10 minutes of daily writing meditation.

Though studies have not yet confirmed it, I suspect that writing meditation can have an even more immediate impact in overcoming loneliness than meditation. I've seen people become more social and outgoing in just a matter of days. Now, imagine what you can achieve doing both.

Mind, Body and Spirit - The Study of Transpersonal Psychology

Do you like being self employed, studying to human mind, working with people and solving their problems? If so, a career as a psychologist may be for you. However, psychology is such a broad field how should you decide what to focus on?

A general degree in psychology will allow you to study the human mind and human behavior. However, a specific focus allows psychologists to specialize in a number of different areas within the psychology field. Psychologists apply their knowledge to a wide range of areas such as health and human services, management, education, law and sports.

Most common specializations include clinical psychology, counseling psychology, education psychology, school psychology, sport psychology, criminal psychology and child psychology. A far less known specialization is transpersonal psychology. This area of psychology presents a number of challenges and may be an interesting and very rewarding career.

Transpersonal psychology degree programs integrate psychological concepts, theories and methods with spiritual disciplines. This type of degree program will allow you to study spiritual experiences, mystical states of consciousness, rituals as well as states such as psychosis and depression. These programs cover the full range of human experiences, from abnormal behavior to normal and spiritually driven actions.

Transpersonal experiences go beyond the limitations of time and space. As a result, transpersonal psychology dives deep into consciousness studies, spiritual inquiry, the body-mind relationship and transformations.

Transpersonal Psychology Degree Programs

Degree programs in transpersonal psychology focus on developing an understanding in the background and tradition of transpersonal psychology and its development and evolution.

Courses covered by these degree programs are broad and varied. They include topics such as counseling theories, strategies and skills, personality theories, contemporary consciousness teachings, theories and practice of meditation, eastern and western strategies for transformation, cross-cultural counseling, and legal issues in counseling. Common elective courses include art and spirituality, conscious living, conscious relationships, death and dying, grief and loss, ecopsychology as well as hypnotherapy, human sexuality and gestalt therapy.

Careers in Transpersonal Psychology

With this degree you could work in academics, focusing on teaching, research or both. You could also work as a part-time faculty member as well as perform counseling and advisor work. Graduates of transpersonal psychology programs run community healing programs, staffing in hospice facilities, provide communication training to schools and business as well as higher education administration and business coaching.

With this degree you could embark on a career in a number of different areas such as education, business, social service, health care and community development.

Mindfulness - For Business People?

It may be the the most important thing you can do. Victor Frankl, in his book about his time in a concentration camp, talks about how a focus on the present helped him to deal with the discomfort of his immediate situation without being overwhelmed by the horror of his life as a prisoner of the Nazi's. Bhuddist teacher Thich Nhat Hanh emphasises being in the moment in his book, "The Miracle of Mindfulness". And Deepak Chopra cites 'Present Moment Awareness" as one of the "Seven Spiritual Laws of Success".

What is 'Being Fully Present'

A state of consciousness. A state of mind. A way of being. Being in the zone. Mindfulness. Whatever you call it, 'being fully present' means that you are fully absorbed and committed to what you are doing - NOW.

It is also probably true that being fully present can be a different experience for each of us, and indeed that it can be a changing experience for each of us. This implies that Being Fully Present can be a qualitative experience - factors can change how we experience it: Practice improves and deepens the experience and makes it easier; our state when we 'go into it' can affect the state we go into; it is a skill we can develop.

What are the benefits of Being Fully Present? What's in it for you?

To answer that question we need to consider it from a number of perspectives:

1. Your Life Will Have Meaning and Purpose

The philosophical, existential perspective. Consider your life as a conscious experience. Is it not true that the only conscious experience that you can have is the one that you are having now? And would that not lead to the idea that your life is being lived, now? That all of life is now?

So if we are not focused and completely giving ourselves to the present moment, are we not living a lesser experience, a watered down life? Don't you want to live your life to the full?

2. You are More Likely to Have What you Want.

Without focus on the present moment, we are less likely to succeed. If you do things with 50% of your mind on the task at hand and 50% somewhere else, you are less likely to get the quality of output - the result - you want. I know when I do this I usually end up being dissatisfied with my work. And, being a bit of perfectionist, that can mean that I don't want to use the output, which means that I have completely wasted my time. I needn't have bothered at all. How many times have you done something in a half-hearted way, put it down and never gone back to it? Or junked what you have done and started all over again? Each time you do this is a lost opportunity. If you focus on the task at hand, you will do it better. And if you are doing something at all, don't you want it done as well as possible? If you can do whatever you are doing to the best of your ability you are far more likely to succeed.

Now I feel the need to come in here and say that I am not referring here to the creative process. My creative process is often that I start something more than once, go round in circles, and generally look like I am wasting time and effort. What I have discovered about myself is that this is all a natural function of my creative process and is ok, even necessary. The point is, even while I am doing stuff that I don't use, I am doing it with full awareness and concentration.

3. We Are More Likely to Have the Relationships We Want.

Deep, meaningful relationships that enrich our lives and the lives of those we share with. In fact, being fully present in my primary relationships is the only way I have found to sustain them. (I then have to add the dimension of being there for the other person, so that my focus is on them not on me. But I couldn't do that until I was able to ground myself).

Perhaps the hardest lessons I have learned about living fully in the moment relate to relationships. I have been married twice and experienced many more relationships, and I can honestly say that if I had been living in the moment (for most of my life I didn't know about this at all, so that wasn't really an option to me except when I did it unconsciously, without trying) I could still have been in any one of those relationships successfully and happily.

4. Peace of Mind

Mindfulness allows you to be aware of what is happening, without being drawn into it emotionally. With mindfulness, you can maintain calmness of mind and choice of thought. If negative thoughts arise, you can divert your thoughts to more positive thoughts that garner good feelings. Say to yourself. "I want to feel good!"

'What you focus on, you become. So always focus on that which is the highest, brightest, happiest and most Noble of all Things - Enlightenment.'

Rama

The detachment that can come with mindfulness helps you to remain calm in the midst of a storm. When something unwelcome or unexpected happens, there can be a tendency for the mind to become overwhelmed. This is triggered by a rush of brain chemicals and rapid activity in the brain. Immediately following this 'rush', you have a choice: reach for mindfulness or continue with the mental turmoil. With mindfulness you can find clarity of thought and rational decision making. Even better, you will reduce the stress of the moment. Reducing stress in the moment is a good outcome. The long term cumulative benefits to your health and emotional well-being of a reduction in stress are considerable.

How to Attain Mindfulness

There are many books and other resources to help you to become mindful. Here are some suggestions:

Meditate.

Meditation allows your inner self through. If you meditate by connecting to your breathing, using a mantra, or connecting your body in some other way by watching your body you are developing your abilities to observe and detach.

Focus on your breathing.

When you don't have anything in particular to concentrate on, or if the reverse is true and your mind is so full of 'stuff' you can't think straight, pull back from all of that, and just concentrate on your breathing. There's no need to change or alter your breathing, just give your full attention to it. Follow it. Notice how concentrating on your breathing brings you back to earth, quietens your mind and slows your body functions down.

Concentrate fully on whatever activity you are engaged in.

Thich Nhat Hanh suggest that 'when you are washing the dishes, be only washing the dishes'. Give your full concentration to the activity of washing the dishes. You may find that time seems to slow down and calmness sets in.

Be before you do.

Another way to say this is 'Be Do Have'. Before you launch yourself into an activity, consider your mental and physical state. What is going on now in your body? How is your breathing? Are your muscles tight and bunched, or loose and relaxed? How do you want your body to be for this activity?

What is going on with your thoughts? Are you thinking about what you want to think about, and in a state of mind likely to enable this activity, or hinder it? Are you fully aware?

Develop your Mind/Body Connection.

Using your awareness, and in a specific order, scan your body. You might start at the tips of the toes of your left foot and work up your left foot, your left ankle, your lower leg and so on in a similar way all the way up to your left hip. When you get to an area that doesn't feel how you want it to, pause and think about the feeling you want to have in that area until it starts to arrive there. Then move on, slowly. Pay particular attention to muscles and joints in your limbs, and to your organs in your torso. When scanning your head, pay attention to the muscles of your face and neck, and your scalp. If you sit down to practice this, you may fall asleep, it's so relaxing!

If you are sitting down, you can augment this by noticing the feel of the chair underneath your buttocks and the ground on your feet.

This practice will bring you back to the present moment and is very grounding.

Want to improve your Sales Performance? if you are a Sales Manager who wants your team to perform better, increase your Direct Sales or Channel Sales revenues and make your sales more profitable, Robert Neely can help you.

Mind-Reading Creates Confusion in Relationships

Did you know that mind-reading is at the root of a lot of communication problems in relationships? Recently I read statistics about the accuracy of mind reading. I was not surprised to read that studies showed that close friends and couples read each other right only 35% of the time.

Couples, especially the ones who have been together for several years, fall easily into the mind-reading habit. They assume that they each know what the other one is thinking without really checking it out. Certainly many times these guesses will be accurate but as we see from the above statistics 65% of the time they are wrong. Mind-reading where one person is sure he/she knows what the other person is thinking, restricts honest communication.

No doubt you have heard the tale of the tuna casserole or something similar. The wife keeps making tuna casserole weekly to please her husband only to find out 20 years later that he never liked tuna casserole. She 'knew' he liked tuna casserole and he tolerated it because he 'knew' that she loved tuna casserole. I do not remember how they finally let each other know that they disliked tuna casserole. 20 years is a long time to put up with something that could easily have been cleared up years earlier by talking about it.

The 'tuna casserole' tale is also a good example of relationship balance. Here are two people whose intentions are good because each is concerned about pleasing the other. Unfortunately, they wasted many years tolerating the casserole instead of eating with pleasure. If they had honestly shared their feelings about the tuna casserole they probably would have found ways to create meals that both truly enjoyed.

In relationships it is important to stay away from mind-reading. Over the years I have worked with many couples and have heard one or the other say " my partner just doesn't get me. Mind-reading,instead of direct open communication, may well be going on in such a relationship.

Here are four truisms to remember about mind-reading:

1. No one else can read your mind.

2. You alone know what you are thinking and feeling

3. Others can guess and will be right some of the time

4. When you see it differently, speak up

Mind-reading can be a communication short-cut and useful as long as both partners take responsibility to speak up when there is a discrepancy between the mind-reading assumption and what is really going on.

Mindfulness-Based Marriage & Couples Therapy

Relationships are hard, and a successful marriage needs to be a joint endeavour in which both parties are fully committed to managing and resolving conflicts and emotional upsets as they arise. This is a skill and life-long journey, and one of the best tools that can help you negotiate the many emotional problems that will arise in a marriage or other family relationship is the skill of mindfulness.

We all tend to become locked into patterns of habitual reactivity and fixed points of view. We all become experts in what is right and wrong, good and bad, and we impose these beliefs on each other. We have demands and expectations that we "know" are completely right, and impose these on our partner. However, relationships do not respond to demands and expectations or any other from of behavior designed to control another. Relationships thrive on communication, and for communication to be effective there must be freedom and openness based on trust and compassion. The only way to establish this quality of freedom is for each partner to take responsibility for his or her emotional reactions and learn to resolve them so that they do not corrupt communications. Emotional reactivity causes the mind to contract and become fearful and this inhibits effective communication and problem solving. We all know the importance of getting in touch with our feelings, but how do we do this, and what do we do when we have gotten in touch with our fear, anxiety, anger, disappointment or hurt?

In Mindfulness Meditation Therapy, whether given in the Office or through Skype sessions, the focus is on teaching you how to work with your inner feelings and how to establish a relationship with them that facilitates healing, transformation and resolution. Mindfulness is a particular form of focused awareness that can be described as "engaged-presence." We choose to engage rather than avoid or deny our inner pain. We choose to engage with our hurt rather than blaming it on our partner or some other external cause. We change our focus from, "I am angry because... ," to "I am angry," and then further refine this into, "I notice anger within me." With each shift, we begin to change our relationship with our anger, or any other emotion, such that it becomes an object that we can relate to. This is the first part of what it means to get in touch with our feelings.

The second part of "getting in touch" is to learn to be present with our inner pain or hurt. Being present means listening with an open mind and an open heart and being willing to "sit" with our feelings without trying to fix them, resist them or do anything other than be still and open with a mind intent on listening and being aware. Mindfulness is the art of listening in this way, and creating a therapeutic space around inner suffering that is imbued with natural love and compassion. When you begin to relate to your pain in this way, it responds in kind and begins to unfold, unclench, unwind and loosen its grip on you. This is what promotes healing and the resolution of the emotional component of your problem. Heal this and you will find it much easier to resolve the objective components to the problems.

Really, learning to relate to another begins when you learn how to relate to your inner self, those emotional beings that reside within your mind. The two cannot be separated, and when you learn to love yourself, it is then that you will know how to love another. Mindfulness provides the skillful means to achieve both.

CONCLUSION

The term sounds easy enough to comprehend, but there is a much deeper meaning. Terms like mindfulness and loving-kindness seem obvious, but you have to understand them before you can implement them, into your daily life.

This reminds me of a conversation I, recently, had with a friend. He was reading the personal ads, in the singles section, and came across another term: "consciously aware." He was grasping to understand why so many women had listed this as a prerequisite to any kind of relationship, with a male companion.

When he mentioned this to me, and I could see the puzzlement all over his face, I couldn't suppress a smile. I asked him, "Are you a good listener?" Now, he was completely "thrown off the track."

So, I explained that women, who had been exposed to men, who didn't listen, had written these advertisements. Living in the moment, and being consciously aware, are components of mindfulness.

Therefore, let's take an in-depth look at the meaning of mindfulness. Staying in the present moment is, probably, the hardest part, for most of us. We spend so much time thinking about the past and future, that there is little time to see life, as it is.

Imagine, what would happen, if you drove a car like that. Looking over your shoulder, and blocks ahead, most of the time, would get you into an accident. Due to the fact, you were not aware of what is right in front of you. So what do you do?

Let's take the first step together today. Firstly, make a commitment to create the daily habit of mindfulness. After that, start to listen to the world around you and the world within you. The universe is outside, and within, at the same time. This is proven by the fact that the universe is infinitely vast and infinitely small.

Now, back to listening to yourself. Make it a point to notice how often you are nervous, tense, or distracted, and learn to focus on your breath. Breath awareness will calm your inner being, and you can do it anytime. If you want to learn more about breathing for your overall health, you should attend a workshop or a Yoga class.

Learn to be silent and learn to speak up at the "right time." When is there a right time to speak? Learn to relax before talking. Never speak to inflame a conflict, but do not become silent when you can resolve a conflict. Never be afraid to compromise, and find common ground, with a perceived opponent.

Always remember: The solutions to your problems are all within your own mind.

A man who is stressed is no lover. A woman who is needy, is no partner. A friend who is in crisis is no friend and parents who are always busy are not really doing their job. It is so easy to let life dictate our destiny. So, a little mind control can go a long way.

Thanks You!!!

Writing this book was the real way. And as each path had exciting parts and moments of labor and milk. Fortunately, I was on my way in the comedy by a group of talented, welcoming and friendly life. I'd like to thank them.